I0823059

THE BOOK THAT TAUGHT THE WORLD TO ORGASM AND THEN DISAPPEARED

THE BOOK THAT TAUGHT THE WORLD TO ORGASM AND THEN DISAPPEARED

SHERE HITE AND THE HITE REPORT

ROSA CAMPBELL

MELVILLE HOUSE
BROOKLYN • LONDON

The Book That Taught the World to Orgasm
and Then Disappeared : Shere Hite and the Hite Report

First published in 2026 by Melville House

First Melville House Printing: January 2026
Distributed by Penguin Random House LLC, 1745 Broadway, New York, NY 10019 USA. www.penguinrandomhouse.com

Melville House Publishing
46 John Street
Brooklyn, NY 11201
and
Melville House UK
Suite 2000
16/18 Woodford Road
London E7 0HA

mhpbooks.com
@melvillehouse

ISBN: 978-1-68589-231-9
ISBN: 978-1-68589-232-6 (eBook)

Library of Congress Control Number: 2025949798

Designed by Beste Doğan

Printed in the United States of America
10 9 8 7 6 5 4 3 2 1

A catalog record for this book is available from the Library of Congress

The authorized representative in the EU for product safety and compliance is Easy Access System Europe, Mustamäe tee 50, 10621 Tallinn, Estonia. gpsr.requests@easproject.com

CONTENTS

PROLOGUE

In 1972, Shere Hite, *Playboy* model turned feminist sex researcher, jumped on a motorbike and drove around Manhattan. With apricot curls and a vintage lace gown streaming out behind her, she handed out surveys to any woman who would take one. This was no ordinary survey. It was all about sex. Across fifty-eight questions, Shere asked women how they did it, how they felt about it, and what gave them the greatest pleasure. She asked women to describe how it felt to orgasm 'or do a drawing'. She asked what they thought of their vaginas ('ugly or beautiful?'), and whether they thought 'sex was in any way political?' She explained her rationale: 'As women it is time we defined our own sexuality—what it feels like, how we have experienced it, what we want from it'.

Completed surveys and letters flooded in to Shere, first from women in New York, then from all across the United States and around the world. Women's responses offered granular, highly detailed personal accounts that hummed with feeling. They contained drawings of women having sex; one woman drew concentric circles approximating the 'delicious' feeling of an orgasm. They were written in different coloured pens, and in a great range of handwriting. As women filled it out, they pushed the pen hard into the page with anger, or added a flourish under 'orgasm'. One woman had commandeered the work typewriter, answered it a bit at a time and 'hurried home . . . horny, horny, horny'. Another had hidden the survey as she filled it out and quickly sent it back to Shere. She wished she could keep a copy for herself but was worried her husband would find it. This 'would hurt him too much and I can't do that to him, he has been good to me'.

These responses became *The Hite Report: A Nationwide Study of Female Sexuality*, the 1976 smash-hit bestseller and one of the most popular, important, and overlooked feminist books of the twentieth century. The great provocation of *The Hite Report* was that most American women were wildly sexually dissatisfied. Seventy percent of women did not reach orgasm during sex without clitoral stimulation, though most women's sex lives did not include much of this and they didn't ask for it. Women fucked through gritted teeth or faked orgasms—the loudest way of being silent about sexual dissatisfaction: 'Do I fake? Like asking if the sky is blue', wrote one woman. 'I used to do the whole B-movie scene with groans and everything', wrote another.

To understand why women's sex lives were so abysmal and why most women put up with this, and maintained their silence at great cost to themselves, Shere held sex up to feminism. Looking at it in this way, in this light, she found that sex was shot through with power and inequality. Society insisted that women, like men, should find their greatest pleasure in penetrative sex: the woman penetrated, the man penetrating. Shere declared 'sex is sexist . . . Women's sex lives very clearly reflect their second-class position in the society. Women, still, in 1976 make only 60% of the amount men make for the same work: men have a right to more rewards (money, services, respect) than women. Just so in sex'.

But Shere knew from her own extraordinary life before *The Hite Report* that sex didn't just *reflect* the inequalities of the world, it generated them. The bedroom was a crucial site of women's oppression, as important as the factory floor, the court, the hospital, the kitchen, the nursery, the House of Representatives. She was one of the first to see sex in this way, and she popularized this insight and made it accessible to millions across the world. *The Hite Report* is the thirtieth-bestselling book of all time; other books about women that have sold as many copies include *Lolita* and *Anne of Green Gables*.[1] Yet, compared to these storied titles, barely anything has been written about *The Hite Report*. The book's impact and how it changed sex globally has not been charted. I do that here, across these pages.

Without *The Hite Report*, there would be no understanding, now common sense, that great sex means pleasure for all involved. It is difficult to imagine a time when we did not use our own experience and feelings to determine whether sex has gone well or badly, but we owe this to Shere. Without her book, there would be no imperative that women speak up about what they want in sex, no knowledge of the clitoris as important for women's pleasure, no sparkling anatomical vagina Christmas decorations to hang on the tree in place of the angel, the bell-as-clitoris jingling away. Without *The Hite Report*, there would be no raging trade in feminist sexual self-help or sex toys designed to maximise women's pleasure that can now be bought with ease, online during some stolen seconds at work or while doing the weekly grocery run, your choice of vibrator sitting beside the frozen peas in the trolley.[2] Without *The Hite Report*, there would have been no *Sex and the City*, a show based on women talking in explicit, confessional detail about sex, a form Shere's book popularised. Nor would Meg Ryan have faked her orgasm over a pastrami sandwich in the first-ever rom-com, *When*

Harry Met Sally, demonstrating a key finding of Shere's to Billy Crystal: While he was sure women never faked it during sex with him, 'most women at one time or another have done it, so you do the math'.

Long before the #MeToo movement encouraged women to share story after wretched story publicly to show how prevalent sexual violence is in so many of our lives, Shere compiled stories from survey responses, not of assault and rape, necessarily, but certainly of bad, unpleasurable sex, to create a picture of how sex worked. The thousands of letters she received from women often said the literal words 'me too', and they expressed a similar relief, 'I am so glad to know it is not just me'. Today we talk about the orgasm gap, naming how in straight sex women have far fewer orgasms than men. Research published in 2020 suggested that this was due to 'our cultural prioritization of penile-vaginal intercourse' over 'clitorally focused sexual activities'.[3] To close this gap, researchers suggest tearing up cultural scripts that equate sex with vaginal penetration and instead include clitoral stimulation as standard. Shere made these suggestions in 1976.

Initially, *The Hite Report* exploded across the United States. For a time, Shere Hite was everywhere; if you opened a newspaper or switched on the TV in the mid-1970s, you might well have seen her talking very seriously about feminism and sex, her eyes peeping out under a mane of strawberry-blond curls. If you turned the dial on the radio, her lilting voice might have filled your kitchen as she talked about 'the clitoris' and 'the orgasm'. She did thousands of media appearances when *The Hite Report* first came out, and the book was written up in newspapers across the United States. She did her own publicity, and she was relentless. At first, the press loved her: She was an ex-model, she was beautiful, her style was unique and highly feminine, she wore purple pineapple-print shirts, a manicure, sparkling vintage costume jewellery, and a full face of makeup. She didn't look the way they expected a feminist to look, and she talked about sex all the time. Shere's media work took feminism into the bedrooms of the suburbs, under the sheets of beds with quilted covers, into factories where women read the book on their lunch breaks, and into the lives of men working on drilling rigs, in prisons, reading *Playboy*. The book resonated with women globally, and her status as a hot American celebrity meant the book travelled widely and was translated quickly. The story of Shere Hite and *The Hite Report* changes the stories we tell about feminism; it is usually presumed that men and suburban women were not touched by this movement. Feminist movements are still largely discussed within the national context—we talk about U.S. feminism, Italian feminism, Indian feminism, for example—but feminist ideas cross borders, and the history of *The Hite Report* shows us how. To chart this history, I use the thousands of letters Shere received from women and men in the United States and around the world. No one except Shere Hite has read these letters before.

Despite the impact of *The Hite Report* across the United States and around the world, the book is not well known today. I told many of my friends that I was writing a book about *The Hite Report* and Shere Hite. Mostly they shrugged: 'Who's that?' And yet, I know that their sex lives are indebted to Shere, as mine is. In compendiums of feminist political thought, or histories of the U.S. movement, *The Hite Report* is rarely included, and Shere does not feature in any collections where prolific feminists offer reflections on the movement.[4] But the book outstripped other feminist blockbusters by millions, sometimes tens of millions, of copies. It's hard to imagine how a book like this could be wiped from public memory, but as opposition to feminism grew, so did opposition to Shere. Initially, the book was lauded by everyone from the *New York Review of Books* to *Cosmopolitan*. Even *Penthouse* was relieved that in this 'startling' book 'women are finally speaking out for themselves'. But as attacks on Shere grew, her work became known as 'The Hype Report', 'Sheer Hype', and 'Sheer Shite'.

Throughout my research, I often asked people why they thought the media had gone after Shere. Perhaps, they suggested, it was an inevitable celebrity rise-and-fall story, where dizzying heights of fame give way to a plunge at least as fast and steep? Or they would say something like 'feminist knowledge is always being suppressed, that's patriarchy for you'. I too am a feminist, but I found this explanation unsatisfying. It obscures at least as much as it illuminates. I was left wondering exactly *how* this silencing works. It can't just be inevitable; otherwise, all us feminists might as well pack up and go home now. It also didn't explain why the media went for Shere rather than Gloria Steinem, who was perhaps just as famous. Or why it was Shere rather than Andrea Dworkin, who also talked about sex and power, women and men, but in much more strident terms than *The Hite Report* ever did. Paying close attention to Shere's story and the story of *The Hite Report* helps us see how this kind of silencing works. I get under the skin of the spinning, punning headlines and situate these attacks on Shere in the backlash against feminism in the 1980s. Across the 1960s and 1970s, feminists did change society, and they faced a shadow movement of those whose power was threatened. This was not inevitable but political. Through focussing on Shere, I also show how the backlash felt, how one woman lived it, and how she came undone.

I CALL HER ***SHERE*****, NOT** to diminish her standing as a thinker or her impact but to reflect the amount of time I have spent with her. *The Hite Report* was the first book about sex I ever read. My parents, 1970s radicals, had a copy. Even though it posed as a serious report, black and red letters on a white cover, somehow I knew that it was a book of revelations. It seemed to wink at me, exude a sexual aura, promise something illicit. I read it aged ten; I found it shocking, and I found it erotic, and I never forgot it. I was too young, but better this as a sexual entrée than internet porn. When I began to study global feminist history, this early reading experience floated to the front of my mind. Shere 'intruded on the privacy of my bath, joined me in the ocean', as historian Blanche Wiesen Cook warns that those we study sometimes do.[5] Like a siren, Shere beckoned me into her own sea. She suggested I do a project about her. I might go to her archive, swim in her words, and put them together with mine. So I did, and she came alive to me.

Via her archives, her books and papers, Shere and I have discussed a lot, sometimes disagreeing quite passionately. I hope I have listened hard to her. As I read her dream recollections, where the spectres of her very difficult childhood haunted her, so too she invaded my dreams. My style subtly shifted across the project, a lace collar here, a pussy bow and a glossed lip there. I grew my hair out. People asked me if I liked her, and honestly, I still don't know. What I do know: She often took my breath away. In the silent Schlesinger Library, I would gasp, in awe of her determination, of how well she did against an early life of real hardship and poverty, of how she managed through sheer grit to take feminist ideas as wide and far as possible. Other times, I would let out a groan and think to myself, *Oh God, no she didn't.*

Sometimes I felt like I'd been set up, like she had been waiting for someone to write this book and I was the sucker. Her archive is expansive, with nearly three hundred boxes, but it's also heavily curated. There are folders called 'my private moments and most forbidden thoughts', really only labels you write if you want someone else to read them. She kept recordings of many of her media appearances, but none of the ones where she behaved less than graciously. She saved every single one of her newspaper and magazine interviews, articles, and reviews; any mere mention of her name was clipped and filed. There are thousands and thousands of these. She organised her archive to make her look good, to tell the story of a visionary feminist and then a woman scorned. But, despite her efforts, a lot slipped through. There is more to the story than this. Where were her friends, I wondered. I expected hundreds of letters from feminists, and they were not there. Why did the National Organization for Women sue her? Why did she punch a limo driver? Why did it sometimes seem like her own redemption was bound up in the success of her work? That she would do anything to keep the spotlight on her, anything at all to make the world love her?

I HOPE CALLING HER SHERE does not stop me from being fearless and critical where necessary. Like many white feminists of the 1970s, her race politics leave a lot to be desired. When she says 'women' she means white women, but that is never made explicit; instead, the particular experience of white women is presumed to be the experience of all women in the United States. In *The Hite Report*, there is no discussion of race, and as women of colour feminists have written, this was typical of the women's liberation movement at that time.[6] When Shere's book travels to the Global South on the coattails of American power, her feminism is imperialist, and she sees women in need of uplift by their white American sisters. I don't minimise these flaws in this book or downplay these faults. Sometimes she teaches us what not to do. Regardless, I don't think that we should discard her work, because to do that would stop us from learning from her. Indebted to work by historian Clare Hemmings and scholar-activist Loretta Ross, I think sometimes our critiques of feminists of an earlier period are used to demonstrate that we have it figured out and are now effortlessly intersectional, in both word and deed.[7] Our critiques are delivered in a mode of 'suspicion, self-confidence and indignation', to show that unlike women in the past, we know how to integrate questions of race and racism into our feminism, along with all other axes of oppression, and how to act after the analysis to take back the power.[8] If only this were true. As Ross tells it, this protects the ego, but it's a fantasy. The times we live in show us as much.

Shere's ideas about sexual liberation and how feminism might lead us there seem so relevant today when the U.S. president is a predator, a rapist elected not once but twice. The story of Shere Hite and *The Hite Report* is useful because we too are facing a period of global backlash, characterised by resurgent misogyny, homophobia, transphobia, and racism. In the wake of movements for gender justice, including the global #MeToo movement and agitation for the rights and freedoms of transgender and queer people and the movement for Black lives, and compounding crises since the 2008 economic crash, including the pandemic and the climate crisis, the political right has doubled down, exploiting anxiety and sowing division. Today, the global right works to bring in a world where bodies are immutable and biologically determined by sex, and where men and women are in a 'natural' hierarchy. They see the patriarchal family as sacred, and the nation as bordered, ordered, militarised, and racially homogenous. They seek to restore a mythical past when this was allegedly true. This is a vision shared globally by those at the very top of institutional politics from the United States to India to Turkey, as well as those powering far-right grassroots movements. This includes the manosphere's most famous misogynist, Andrew Tate, and tradwife influencers, communities of right-wing, "traditional wife" women who advocate through social media for hierarchical gender roles where men hold social and political power and women are confined to the home.

It can seem that this particular moment in history is unprecedented, and that makes it hard to know what to do. But Shere faced something similar; indeed, some of the ideas present in today's version of the backlash can be found in this earlier moment. To push back today, we need to develop more specific understandings of how backlashes work. The history I lay out might help. The story I tell might assist us in coming up with moves to counter the times we face and to accrue power. We might use the original analysis of sex that Shere offered or her vision of liberation as an inspiration to take back what is ours. Perhaps she can teach us something about how we might reach millions of people unconvinced of our politics, which we certainly need to do. Shere Hite taught me that feminism is a movement for survival, for pleasure and for liberation for women, certainly, and for everyone else. It is my hope that across these pages you will find that too.

CHAPTER 1
WHAT SHERE HITE KNEW

The papers of Shere Hite are stored at the Schlesinger Library on the History of Women in America at Harvard University. I first visited the day after Donald Trump was elected for the second time. The library is neat as a pin. It has chocolate-coloured bricks, big Georgian windows, and white accents, like icing on a gingerbread house piped by someone with a very steady hand. It was once part of Radcliffe College, where women were educated and excluded from Harvard until it went coed.

Despite the tragedy of a second Trump presidency, I skipped up the steps, excited to meet Shere through the more than 280 boxes in her archive. In the reading room, I waited at the large wooden table, the ceiling high, the room flooded with light from the blue, blue day. I sat, quiet and reverential, in this hushed temple of women's rights, portraits of feminist foremothers looming above me. The archivists brought Shere to me on a trolley, one box and then the next and the next. I started at the very beginning, with box one, dedicated to biographical material.

I had questions. I wanted to know why it was Shere who had written *The Hite Report*. How did Shere know that sex and power were tangled together, that, as she wrote on the first page, 'a woman's place in sex mirrors her place in the rest of society'? What, in her life before the book, had taught her this?

The first manila folder felt lumpy and bulging. I opened it to find a clotted pile of notes. Post-its, which I soon learnt Shere favoured, were stuck together with scribblings, on envelopes, on notepaper pulled from jotters, on the individual paper cases each Earl Grey tea bag came in. She wrote on small, sometimes tiny pieces of paper; on one shred, she has scribbled 'women!' The notes are arranged by time, in months and years, not by theme, so they are a record of what crossed her mind. One pile includes: 'apologize', 'I love the sound of your voice', 'dye the curtains green myself', along with ideas for projects: 'humiliation in plots', 'What's new? How masculinity traps men'. She had a very distinctive hand, copperplate writing with beautiful flourishes and embellishments. She often wrote in fine-point felt pen in green or black. Martin Sage, her boyfriend in the 1970s, had partly been wooed by a letter she had written him. He said when we spoke: 'If the word "cursive" means anything, it means her handwriting'.

Beneath the tower of notes, there were pages and pages of typed and handwritten scripts; letters, drafts of articles, ideas she was thinking through. Often she wrote on hotel stationery, of the Paris Hilton, the UN Plaza Hotel in New York, or on her own letterhead, *Hite Research Institute* in cursive under winged deer in flight, all embossed in gold. Each page is a collage. She typed her notes, then corrected them by hand, stuck on other paragraphs of text, sometimes added photos and scrawled notes and to-do lists in the margins. These pages have the maximalism of a riot grrrl zine, the bloat of a scrapbook.

Present too are traces of her high femininity. Among the papers, there are fabric samples for clothing she got made-to-measure, after *The Hite Report* made her rich. As I ran my finger over a small square of fine floral silk and a patch of olive velvet, I felt as if I were tugging on her sleeve and asking her all my questions. There was a napkin where she had blotted her lipstick and taken copious notes about the role of women in opera. Joanna Briscoe, her partner in the 1990s, recalled that Shere always took notes at dinner, then wrapped her leftover steak in the paper serviette, putting it in her handbag for later. Sometimes I felt sure I caught her scent on the breeze, expensive face powder and a warm floral note, a little stale now. I would turn my head to try to get a more fulsome whiff, but she always disappeared. Once, a glossy blond hair slipped out, was held glimmering in the autumnal sunshine, and drifted onto the desk. She was all around me, tiny particles of her in the air, her skin, her dust, her paper, my hands. Shere, Shere, everywhere.

As I made my way through folder after folder, learning to clasp each one with both hands to stop any bits and pieces of her falling to the floor, a picture started to appear. Putting together her life as a young girl in St. Joseph, Missouri, as a teenager learning to perform femininity in Daytona Beach, Florida, as a graduate student at Columbia University, then working as a model in fashion and porn in New York, it became clear that before her most important book, the first *Hite Report*, she experienced four distinct sexual cultures. This allowed her to look over the top and grasp the role sex played in America, its relationship to power, and how this most private matter structured the public sphere and maintained gender equality. It made *The Hite Report* a book only she could write.

THERE WAS AN EARTHQUAKE THE day Shere Hite was born, on November 2, 1942. Her mother named her Shirley Diana Gregory. She was born in St. Joseph, Missouri, population seventy-five thousand. Here the corn grew high, the pigs fat, and the ruddy, red Jonathan apples were celebrated each spring with a famous parade. The local tremor almost didn't make the news; the nation was at war, and the *St. Joseph Gazette* was given over to international reports of the United States 'smashing and pounding' and 'cutting the enemy down' and 'dealing a severe blow' to the Japanese. Closer to home, the Boy Scouts were wondering what they would do for their Yuletide toy drive, as all the metal toys had been melted down into bombers to fight Hitler. Odds are that quite a few of those kerchiefed boys collecting broken wooden spinning tops would later read *The Hite Report*, but on the day she was born, *Springtime in the Rockies* played at the cinema, and local residents were urged to keep an eye out for a naughty dog gone missing, 'answers to the name Sin Sin'. Women were invited to do war work, and in segregated St. Joseph, the St. Francis Hotel wanted a 'colored maid', while a family specified a 'white girl for housework and care of children'.

Shere was born in the so-called heartland of America, where national mythologies beat their comforting, nostalgic rhythm of exceptionalism, protection, and localism. The institutions she attended, her school and church, would have been all white, with Black people present only in service roles. The heartland is still seen as 'white, rural and rooted', staunch against an age of global connectedness. As historian Kristin Hoganson remarks, it is 'the quintessential home referenced by "homeland security", the model for an America that conservatives want to Make Great Again.[1] Shere's early life shows us how this allegedly more innocent world was fashioned, who was controlled for others' comfort, who was punished, who the doors of clapboard houses were slammed shut to keep out.

Shere was an illegitimate child born to a teenager. Her mother, Shirley Gertrude Hurt, was a schoolgirl, though she dropped out when she fell pregnant; it was illegal to continue. Her father, Paul Gregory, was conscripted and serving on an army base when Shere was born. He came back to visit once or twice when she was a tiny baby and then left forever. Shere was one of many illegitimate children born during World War II, which shook up sexual norms. Newspapers and government propaganda blamed women for this. The month that Shere was born, a *Newsweek* story focussed on Kansas City, close to St. Joseph, spoke of teenage girls like Shirley who liaised with soldiers, presenting them as prostitutes whose promiscuity spread venereal disease, loosened sexual morals, and so threatened national security.[2]

Shirley's parents agreed. They were fundamentalist Christians who interpreted the Bible as the literal word of God. They felt without this there was only chaos on earth and the tortures of hell for all eternity. Sex was a way for women to show their submission and devotion in marriage, and a way for men to increase their power in the family and the nation, through the production of (white) children. Shirley should have been content canning vegetables, praising God, and sewing costumes for the famous St. Joseph Apple Blossom Festival, like her own mother was. There is a picture of Shirley among Shere's papers. She walks in heels, her coat open, her blouse low-cut. There's a touch of the witch about her, accentuated by a house with a turreted roof and skeleton trees in the background. The photo was taken in strange circumstances, snapped at a moment when Shirley had been caught having illicit sex and was being punished for it. Shere explained, when her mother 'was forced to come home from visiting my father-to-be at his house—probably they were making out there'; her parents went and found her and took the picture on the walk home. 'Funny that they would have taken a picture'. Funny, certainly, where 'funny' means *odd and humiliating.* But Shirley does not look humiliated. She stares right at the camera with one eyebrow and her chin raised, her eyes flashing defiantly. She looks like she finds attempts by society, by the church, and by her parents to control her sexuality a big joke. She does not look like she is going to be canning beans anytime soon.

Shirley might not have been ashamed, but her parents certainly were. There's a photo of Paul and Shirley, who is likely pregnant with Shere, where they look so young and surprised. On the back, Shere's grandmother has written, 'Paul and Shirley . . . neither of them were 20 years. So they failed you and their selves'. 'Failed you' is underlined with a thick black line. I imagine Shirley's parents laid out the options. She could marry Paul, but Paul was not around. She could leave St. Joseph before her pregnancy was showing and travel to a maternity home, where she would give the baby up for adoption, fulfilling the needs of a deserving, white married couple who desperately wanted a child.[3] If she had made this sacrifice and contribution to another white family, she could have returned to St. Joseph redeemed from shame, as if the pregnancy had never happened. Shirley might have known that she could have an illegal abortion, as it was less an issue for fundamentalist Christians in the 1940s, though across this decade abortionists were subject to more police raids, more persecution.[4] But she did none of this, and so, in the eyes of her parents, Shirley embodied degraded sexual morals. She violated the norms of chaste, respectable femininity crucial for the myth of the heartland, the church, and their own family. As they saw it, she needed to be punished severely. They shunned her throughout her pregnancy. She had to be ostracised from the family lest she contaminate them. This was the context baby Shere was born into.

SHIRLEY GAVE BIRTH, THEN SKIPPED town, leaving Shere with her grandparents. They sent her to school and took her to church on Wednesday evenings and Sunday mornings. They kept her fed and well-turned out. They didn't really hug or touch her. They raised her in a home that was eerily quiet. It had thin bare walls and no pictures, just Jesus on the Cross who greeted you at the door, 'slumped there . . . in a perpetual semi-coma . . . the blood trickling from his wounds'. Underneath the crucifix was a bookshelf containing a treasured black leather, gold-stamped Bible. Later, her grandmother would place *The Hite Report* on this sacred shelf. Shere was honoured to be included, but this was years away. If someone described what was to come to her when she was a child, I doubt she would have believed them. It would have seemed like a dream or a fairy tale from *A Child's Garden of Verses*, which her grandmother occasionally read her.

'We were poor', wrote Shere, but 'like most others (before TV?) we didn't think of ourselves as "poor"'. Her grandfather owned a small roofing business. Her grandmother helped out by answering the phone and took in mending to make ends meet. They kept chickens; Shere fed them and collected the eggs. Her grandmother killed one a week for Sunday lunch. Shere would wear her best dress for this meal, her hair curled like Shirley Temple. Her grandmother resented having to bring up another child after raising three of her own, surviving grinding poverty and illness. Her grandmother often reminded Shere that her 'parents went away and didn't take care of me . . . [so] I had to go along with whatever she said since I was a "guest"'. There was a children's home close by, and Shere's grandmother would also remind her that 'if it weren't for me, you'd be in there'. If Shere displeased her grandmother, she would throw up her hands and say, 'You'll turn out just like your mother', someone who deserved to be punished and abandoned, 'a slut in other words'. The stakes were high, and Shere did her best to be 'pleasing, a polite child'. For her good behaviour, she was rewarded at Sunday lunch with 'the little unhatched egg . . . still inside the chicken'. But eating this made Shere feel guilty, as if 'it was something that didn't belong to me'. She often wondered if she was taking too much food and wished she didn't have to eat. When she recalls her dreams as an adult, eggs feature.

To escape her grandmother's tight control, she spent lots of time outside. In the yard, there was a beautiful lilac bush twice as tall as Shere, its fragrance heady and 'delicious', masses of wild mint growing around the water tap, and a fence overgrown with 'luxuriant and abundant' honeysuckle. Shere sucked the milk from the stems. There was a large Spirea bush, with its tight clusters of white flowers, known as a 'bridal wreath', as the supple branches can be shaped into wedding crowns. It was not the human touch she wanted, but she loved to walk barefoot, to have the lilac flowers brush her arms like fragrant purple stars. Sometimes she accompanied her grandfather to work. She would ride with him in his old black Ford, gazing out at cornstalks shooting upward greenly and the yellow haze on the horizon as the husks formed, ready for harvest. 'Seeing hay silos and farmers on their tractors—gave me a feeling of quiet happiness', she wrote later. She lay in the grass by a stream and waited for him as he worked. He took her to lunch on Saturdays. Together they would go to Jerre Anne's cafeteria, where Shere would always have meat loaf, an orange drink, and banana cream pie. Really, like most men of his generation, her grandfather had no idea how to look after a child, or what she needed, but he was the best she had. In a will she drafted in the mid-1970s, she left him her diamond ring, which, knowing her taste, would have been quite the rock.

In 1948, when Shere was six, her grandparents divorced after thirty-five years of marriage, a huge scandal for the time, particularly among their strict Christian community where divorce was a sin. They split because her grandfather was unhappy with her grandmother, who 'didn't like to sleep with him'. People at church took sides, and while it was her grandfather who left, most stood by him. Her grandmother was cast out, her treatment similar to that which she had meted out to her own daughter during her pregnancy with Shere. Sex was allegedly a private matter between two people, but Shere saw how it structured her grandmother's life, how it stopped people from talking to her in the street, in the store. I imagine her grandmother sitting alone in the pews with no one to gossip or swap preserves with, no lemon curd for cucumber pickles, no sewing circle. Shere learnt women's sexuality was controlled by men. If you had too much sex, you could be shunned like her mother was; if you didn't have enough, you could be deserted like her grandmother.

When Shere was nine, her mother returned with a new baby. She showed Shere a 'snapshot of her and a man in a bar', scooped her up, and told her, like a warning, that 'they would all be happy'. The man was Raymond Hite, who her mother had hastily married and who had legally adopted Shere. She took his last name and published all her best-sellers under it. They lived on the outskirts of town. There was no heating, no curtains on the windows, and no furnishings. Shere slept on an army cot. The area had recently been flattened for this new development, all the grass and trees dug up, and the house surrounded with mud, which was especially thick in winter when the snow melted. Her mother 'didn't bother much with what went on at home. She liked to go and see friends for most of the day, or even the evening'. Ray was a truck driver who was not there much, and when he was, he went out of his way to ignore Shere. The only time he spoke directly to her was when she walked in on him in the bathroom accidentally. Stunned at the sight of a grown man peeing, she 'stood dead in her tracks'. He swore at her.

She was left to take care of her brother. She fed him canned peaches in his highchair. She lived on those peaches too, along with lettuce and mayonnaise Wonderbread sandwiches, slices of pink Bologna and gallons of Kool-Aid, which stained her tongue bright red. Shere would walk to the corner store and collect these provisions on credit. She was often scolded for the debt her mother had rung up. She got sick and developed hypoglycaemia, an illness now associated with food insecurity and poverty. She had nightmares and fell down the stairs a lot. But she was free, left alone. 'No one cared if I got my hair cut or what time I went to bed'. She didn't have to go to school, so she went downtown to the cinema. She was 'like an untended but perfectly healthy flower', like the purple prairie clover she would have seen on trips with her grandfather, the honeysuckle and wild mint round the tap in the yard. Shere Hite, wild child.

After a year, her mother was unable to cope. She took Shere back to her grandmother's and left with her baby brother, who Shere missed terribly. At her grandmother's, Shere found out about how women took their anger with men out on each other. Her grandmother's tight control spun into violence. Shere recollected this later: 'She used to brood and brood while sewing . . . staring at her hands while she worked'. Her anger would suddenly become 'wild and ferocious . . . A shadow would come across that beautiful yard'. Her grandmother would scream about the man who had left her, the person she was really angry with, but he wasn't there, so she would turn her rage on Shere—who couldn't leave—saying that she 'was causing trouble, a burden on me, a Christian woman'. Her grandmother began to whip Shere with branches of the Spirea bush. Shere 'refused to show cowardice', to wince, cry, or run away. If her grandmother called her inside from the yard to be beaten, Shere would slow down as she walked toward the house. To maintain her pride, she would 'act as if nothing was happening'. Like her mother in the photo, she refused the humiliation. But she began to 'feel very worthless and unwanted'.

SHE DIDN'T HAVE ANYONE TO tell, and as someone who was poor she learnt her experiences of injustice must be tempered before being shared. She must ask herself, 'What will people think?' She learnt her experiences of hardship, violence, and injustice were likely to rub off on her, to taint her character, because she came from 'a family of no account'. She also realised that as a child, there were 'no choices for me, no options I could choose myself', no way to get what she needed. She reflected as an adult, 'I think every child should have the choice of going to a group-kid home. There should be no questions asked, a child should be given at school the addresses of other possible homes and be told that she or he is always welcome there'.

Her mother came back once, a memory she recalled again and again in diaries, in notebooks, and in her memoir. Shirley took Shere to the swimming pool: 'I thought she'd seen the light about what a neat kid I was'. Her mother wore a black swimsuit that laced up both sides, quite risqué for 1950s St. Joseph, 'extremely daring and sexy', Shere thought. Men followed her mother around the pool, and Shirley was captivated by their admiration. To get her mother's attention Shere jumped in at the deep end, but was in over her head, flailing. 'Mother will be here in a minute to get me, she is a great swimmer, she makes beautiful dives', she thought. But 'nothing was happening'. People tried to alert Shere's mother, but she was enthralled by the attention, 'surrounded by admiring men, chatting, talking and flirting', and did not take any notice of her daughter yelling “Help, Help!” her mouth full of water. Her mother remained unaware when a lifeguard dragged Shere from the pool and didn’t seem to notice when Shere sat on the side, throwing up and shivering. They walked home, Shere limped along spitting out chlorinated water, and didn’t mention it. Shere kept her mother’s silence; she never told her grandparents, knowing that if she did, she would never see her mother again. Here is sex again in this story. Shere learnt that sexual attention could be so mesmerizing it was dangerous. Later, water featured in her dreams too, along with the eggs.

Shere barely saw her mother again. Shirley would soon be admitted to a psychiatric facility and spend the rest of her life in and out of institutions. Shere saw her once as an adult on a trip to St. Joseph in 1971. Shere read Lenin, and met her mother’s new boyfriend, Tom. They all went to Kmart together because ‘Tom want[ed] a gun’. After Shere moved to New York, her family wrote her occasional, euphemistic updates about her mother’s condition. Her aunt told her Shirley had been moved to sheltered accommodation, where they were very strict, and she wouldn’t be able to stay if she refused her pills. Her grandmother wrote that Shirley had moved again, and ‘I hope she can handle her own life, but she is not very stable’. After the first *Hite Report* was published, her mother wrote occasional letters to Shere in jagged capitals about life in institutions. She hoped to be able to live more independently, but wrote, ‘so far I have flunked’. She spent her days painting hundreds and hundreds of biblical scenes, hopeful that they would be illustrations for a children’s book of Bible stories. Shirley asked Shere to help her find a publisher. She begged Shere to ‘Please forgive me for all my wrongs I’ve done to you personally’. On the envelope, she insisted, ‘Please forgive’, the letters descending in size, like a voice going from a shout to a whisper as it ran out of steam.

Shere grew into a teenager. When she turned thirteen, she learnt that she was very pretty. She 'happened to lift [her] head and suddenly there was someone in the mirror—someone who looked like a beautiful adult w[oman] in movies'. She was astonished. 'I began to pay attention to my hair, to think . . . about my exterior self'. This was the start of a 'long road'. Shere began to date, but 'the middle class guys bored me, with their worries about if I was middle class too'. She dated 'tough guys', including one who 'fucked me in his car, I didn't feel any pain—or pleasure—just generalised excitement'. After that, things deteriorated: 'he didn't respect me after the fucking'. Shere's grandfather went to this young man's house, to find out what his intentions were. 'Grpa came back very shaken . . . after this boy had pulled a knife on him'. Her grandmother was very disapproving. She caught Shere making out with a boy, dragged her inside, and said, 'they marry the nice ones, you know'. Eventually, Shere ran away. Her grandmother would hit her, and one night, she slapped her back. She went to her grandfather's house twenty blocks away, the proximity a great humiliation to Shere's grandmother. She told him she was never going back. She stayed with her grandfather for a while and slept on the couch, but his new wife was unhappy with this and refused to eat meals with Shere. He had no idea how to handle Shere's sexuality and, repeating the abandonment of Shere by her mother, sent her to live with relatives she hardly knew. Recalling the time, Shere wrote, 'I'm very sad right now, writing all of this'.

She moved from the Midwest to Daytona Beach, Florida, to live with her aunt Cecile and her uncle Paul, a former champion diver turned businessman. In the move, she jumped a few class brackets, into an upper middle-class milieu. She was thrown into a sexual culture that could not have been more different from St. Joseph's and the expectations of her grandparents' austere Christian household. Shere was acutely aware that it was nice of her aunt and uncle to take care of her: 'They didn't have to after all'. They were kind, but she wondered if they really wanted her to stay or if they were just in it for the room and board her grandfather paid them. So she tried to fulfil their expectations. While at first she stayed in her room and listened to records and read philosophy books, she realised the 'expectation was she date and be popular'. She joined the cheerleading squad and was nominated for homecoming queen. She hoped that she would make them like her, that she could stay.

Like many young women of the 1950s, she learnt that appearances were what mattered, that surfaces determine one's fate. Shere wore a bikini to the beach, and I picture her sitting on the tightly packed Daytona sand, sipping Coke from a green glass bottle through a paper straw. She didn't speak much. She wrote later, 'I didn't seem very bright all those years. I was afraid to say anything because it was always wrong, always made people hate me! So I was obsequious'. Shere, like many others, spent her life walking the impossibly narrow and treacherous path between 'good' and 'bad' girl. As she found, most of the women surveyed for *The Hite Report* were also 'brought up to be "good girls"', meaning forbidden from 'finding out about, explor[ing] and discover[ing] their own sexuality'. As historians show us, the messages teenage girls received were mixed; they were encouraged to pursue a sexuality that pleased boys. At the same time, the culture was obsessed with virginal purity. If they failed to hold off boys' advances or gave in to their own sexual desires, girls absorbed the losses. Girls would lose respectability and risk the only socially sanctioned future: marriage. Shere learnt to be 'all about sex, but without sex'.[5]

Like with the yard and the outdoors at her grandmother's house, Shere found a way out of this tight social order. In her room, she lay on her bed or on the floor and listened to classical music on her record player, which helped her to hear beyond suburban Florida to the big world outside. She wrote, 'I heard other ways of thinking, other kinds of lives and I knew I was not alone'. She dreamt of being a composer, 'like Verdi or Wagner or Rachmaninov! What a seriously gorgeous name'. Her room was also a place where she could feel unhappy. But then she would leave and have to perform poise and popularity. She was 'so acutely aware of the underlying reality' that 'the constant living with two levels made [her] feel very surreal, and unreal, and tired all the time, exhausted with the mental effort'.

She completed her first degree at the University of Florida, her tuition paid for by her grandfather. Her family thought she would be a schoolteacher, but she studied history in the hope that she'd be able to understand the present and answer questions that plagued her across her childhood: 'Why were there so many inequalities? Why were people so often uncaring? Why couldn't everybody have an equal chance?'

IN THE MID-1960S, SHE MOVED to New York for graduate school at Columbia, so chosen 'for idealistic reasons, not because it was an Ivy League'. Shere had learnt in Daytona Beach and St. Joseph that controlling women's sexuality was a way to consolidate power, though she 'hadn't yet figured out how to put all the elements together'. She hoped Columbia might be the place to make sense of this. She proposed a doctoral thesis on how women's sexuality had changed over time. The tuition was huge, so she borrowed money from the government loan programme. She worried that she would never pay it back.

She wanted to study the history of ideas with Jacques Barzun. Barzun was a legend. He had extremely exacting standards and read and remembered everything. A founder of cultural history, he treated all different forms of human expression, from war and statecraft to ghost stories, baseball, and table manners, as equally important 'revelations of a society that produced them'.[6] Barzun invited her to meet, and their meeting is indicative of her time at Columbia. She walked through the long corridors until she came to an empty room painted with green glossy paint. Barzun sat against the back wall at his desk. He had placed a single chair in the centre of the room. This had a small desk attached to the arm for note-taking in lectures, so Shere had to slide in awkwardly. Barzun was, I imagine, unsmiling, and placed his arms expansively behind his head: 'What are you here for?' he asked. She explained, and with practiced politeness asked if he had read her master's thesis. He leant back, relaxed into his chair, and said, 'I did read it'—he leant forward and peered at her—'But I don't believe you wrote it. I'm absolutely sure that they don't have most of those books at the University of Florida'. This was one of Shere's 'first experiences of class prejudice, in addition to gender prejudice, overtly expressed'.

She stuck it out at Columbia for a year in the doctoral programme, but it was tough because of class and gender. Unlike the other grad students, she 'didn't go to Vassar', the elite women's college upstate. She felt different from the others: 'They all knew people who went to Yale . . . [I] didn't even know what Yale was . . . [I] knew it was a school. But not that it was *the* school'. At the time, she wrote that her fellow graduate students didn't believe anyone could be 'intellectual, sophisticated, or, at the base, even a good person if they hadn't gone to one of those schools, or whose family had some connections'. Although 'liberals around her talked a lot about the importance of helping the working class, they didn't seem to know any personally', and she didn't let on. She found the whole thing steeped in sexism. Columbia undergraduate programmes were still men only, and though the graduate school was coed, there were no tenured women professors in the history department when she was there. She was a little early for the strikes that shook the campus in 1968. Women weren't ostracised if they had sex, as they were in St. Joseph, or forced to stifle their own aspirations and dream only of marriage like in Daytona Beach, but at Columbia, what counted as history was hugely limited by sexism. The department understood history to mean things white men had thought and done across time. As a field, the history of ideas still has significant difficulties taking women seriously as people who have ideas, and who have moved history with them, let alone in the mid-1960s when Shere was studying.[7]

SHERE TOOK A LEAVE OF absence and never went back. She had big plans for her life. She knew she could think, and she hoped she might start to work on something. But to stay in New York, she needed money and was now in debt, 'more or less a street urchin'. In 1969, boyfriends advised her to use her looks to make a living. She hoped it would be easy money. She joined Wilhelmina Models, one of the city's top agencies, and a rare woman-run business. The boss, Willie Cooper, was the most photographed model of the 1960s. Most famously, she modelled for the Revlon lipstick shade Cherries in the Snow. In the ads, Cooper is pictured on a white fur rug, her lips a brilliant red. These ads made her an icon, and to make sure everyone remembered just who she was, she hung a large version behind her desk at the agency.

At first, Shere enjoyed modelling. 'It was a good feeling of independence and a challenge', and she felt accepted and wanted. She needed the cash, but she also chose to model for its glamour and because, she wrote, 'It was flattering to hear myself called beautiful'.

Across the final year of the 1960s and into the 1970s, Shere modelled widely. In an ad for an after-bath spray, Vive Le Bain (*long live the bath*), she spritzes behind her knees, a part of the body I never thought to perfume. In a shoot for Samsonite luggage, she ironically played a rich woman, and the copy reads: 'Class. It never goes out of style'. She appeared in many commercial film posters and on the covers of trashy, cheap novels, such as *The Sex Clinic*, about a sexual blackmailer, a nymphomaniac, and an ace gumshoe. Robert McGinnis, famous for the *Breakfast at Tiffany's* poster starring Audrey Hepburn, often did the drawings. McGinnis described Shere as 'his muse', with a 'beautiful snow-white complexion'. Shere, he recalled, was a woman who 'knew how to move her body, to show it off to its best effect'. [8] Most famously Shere featured in a McGinnis poster for the 1971 James Bond film *Diamonds Are Forever*. In the poster, both women who straddle a tuxedoed Bond are based on Shere. On the right she is the redheaded Bond girl, sitting atop a horseshoe-shaped silver probe in a gold bikini, diamonds dripping from her ears and trickling from her palm into the hand of another woman, who is also Shere. On the left she is blond, and she looks coyly past the camera in thigh-high boots. Spaceships, helicopters, and an astronaut surround Bond and the Shere Hites.

Modelling wasn't all glamorous Bond posters, and it certainly wasn't the easy money she hoped it would be. Shere spent most of her free time maintaining a standard of beauty she could get paid for. At the time, she wrote: 'I spent the afternoon at the hairdresser and now I have to do it over again because it's too soft for tomorrow. I break fingernails which require 45 minutes precious time to fix. I am hysterical to spend my time this way'. She wanted to think and do intellectual work, so she 'live[d] for the few minutes I have alone after I quiet down enough to find myself—the few minutes after the exercises & 1000 other things before I fall asleep; then I am happy and want to stay awake'. But modelling demanded a good night's rest. If she wasn't maintaining her body and face, she was hustling for work: 'Today I went to Seventh Ave, walking around there, the world was more than I could take . . . Every day I am like a person without arms, bec. I carry heavy loads in each hand: portfolio and makeup bag . . . Doors hit me in the face. I'm caught in such a horrible trap it is just incredible'.

TO CLAW BACK TIME TO think, she needed to make money fast. The pay was better in porn and there was more demand, less time walking around with your portfolio hoping someone would book you. She answered an advertisement seeking 'Nude Models/Must have good figure/$50 a day', around $350 today. For her first job, she travelled across New York to a dusty warehouse filled with naked people and film equipment. The director asked Shere to take off her clothes. For a moment Shere wondered 'if I could do it . . . but I told myself, "Don't be silly, all you have to do is take them off"'. She stripped and got the role. 'It was a bit part in a grade C porno movie, but it was a job'. This first shoot involved sex with men, women, and couples: 'Some of the scenes called for intimacy with another woman. I thought it would seem strange, but it didn't at all'. She tried to pretend she was an old hand at sex on film, 'so as not to seem naïve and not hurt anyone's feelings by seeming to draw back . . . I didn't want anyone to think I was repelled by them'. The other women were all very nice, 'even sisterly'. She described this first film as 'exhilarating . . . it was great really to see so many naked bodies, all kinds and shapes, and great to be naked with a lot of other people who found it perfectly natural'. After they finished shooting, Shere went out for a sandwich and a cup of coffee. She sat in the café window and watched the people pass by. She 'wonder[ed] at what I had done and [thought] how strange it was that regular life could just go on like that, and no one could see how I had changed'.

Working in porn films required long hours, and Shere found she could make as much money from still photographs. Shere described posing for 'playing cards, for porno papers, and for magazines—wearing garter belts and high heels with black stockings . . . sometimes with wigs on, sometimes with partners and without'. Photos were riskier than film. Often it was just Shere and a photographer doing the shoot at a cheap hotel or in a warehouse. Fewer people meant fewer people to look out for each other. She went to one job where she did as the photographer asked and writhed around on the floor. He stood over her, sweating, until she realised the shoot was a fake. She made her escape, and he yelled insults after her. She figured that he had 'wanted to see/rape? nude women'. While the worst hadn't happened, nothing good had taken place either.

THROUGH HER WORK AS A fashion model, and in porn, Shere learnt how, in a different way, sex was wrapped in power. You could make money, sometimes quite fast money, from having it, or pretending to have it, or being an object of desire that others wanted to have. Modelling, she wrote, 'gave me more spare time than a regular job . . . it taught me I could be freer'. But 'it took a lot out of me too'. The work was gruelling and sometimes dangerous, but beyond her personal experience, she found modelling hard because it hurt others. In pornography, she wrote, her participation in acts that were 'so violent, so depersonalized, and degrading' made it seem that women more generally 'want to be brutalized'. While Shere felt that egalitarian erotica was possible, when pornography was 'the only type of explicit pictures available [it] becomes hard not to think of it as reality'. In particular, the mainstream porn films and mags of the 1970s that Shere starred in focussed on male pleasure. The films ended, almost inevitably, in the money shot: male ejaculation. Women facilitated men's pleasure or were objects to be fucked, and there was very little to their sexuality beyond that. There was absolutely no focus on the clitoris. As Shere saw it, porn didn't just represent the subordination of women, it produced it. It taught those who watched to see sex as an assertion of male power.[9]

But, unlike many feminists who were also anti-porn, Shere didn't exceptionalise porn as uniquely generative of gender inequality and violence against women.[10] Shere saw modelling for fashion and advertising as harmful too, contributing to patterns of oppression. At the time, she wrote: 'Modelling is bad because it reinforces all the stereotyped roles already so damaging in our society: wife, mother, sweetheart, sexpot, girl-child, loud-mouthed bitch. It reinforces in the minds of women everywhere that beauty counts for everything'. The way women and sex were represented in porn, in fashion, and in advertising was political; they did not just reflect desire but created it too. These representations informed how sex went in private because they shaped expectations of sex, of what was desirable and beautiful, who fucked and who was fucked, and the narrative arc sex would take. As one woman told Shere for her *Hite Report*, men she slept with acted like she was 'damned impertinent' if her 'responses weren't programmed exactly like those of mythical women in the classics of porn'. Public representations informed the private sexual imagination, and vice versa, on and on like an ouroboros, the serpent that eats its own tail.

The way I've told Shere's story so far is not the way she recounts her life in her own memoir, *The Hite Report on Shere Hite: Voice of a Daughter in Exile*, written in the millennium year. In this book, she describes her childhood as 'apple blossom time'. She insists, 'strangely, even in the midst of my grandmother's outbursts towards me, my inner happiness continued'. The drafts for that book are held in the archive, and I drew on these as I pieced her life together. Comparing her drafts to the finished book, I witnessed Shere flatten the sad, confused, frightened, and angry writings about her life into something relentlessly, eerily upbeat. I sat there at those big wooden tables and saw as she shook her feelings off the page. When she discussed her mother or her grandmother, there were more redactions, corrections, and Post-its placed over her writing than anywhere else. Shere's grandmother was a 'dominating monster' in her notes, where she often described the fear she experienced as a child, but in the autobiography, she writes, 'But I was happy!' Her grandmother's regular beatings become 'she hit me once or twice'. Her work as a model is also cleaned up, no cheap hotels, no poverty, no exploitation, the only porn she describes doing is 'a torso and breasts shot in soft focus'.

Shere's memoir is an example of what the historian Carolyn Steedman calls an 'enforced autobiography'. As a genre, autobiography rests on several promises: that it is true and it is authentic. But often, this is not the case. Autobiographies, as Steedman reminds us, are often demanded by the state. A life must be recounted in a particular way in order to get much-needed resources. [11] Today, those seeking welfare payments have to craft a life that shows them to be 'responsible jobseekers', down on their luck, dodging stereotypes that paint them as liars and skivers. When women and trans people require abortions or gender-affirming care, they (we) must offer a life narrative to medical professionals that fulfils certain expectations. Women seeking abortions have long had to create narratives about how a baby would be ruinous and send them mad, rather than it just not being the right thing, right now. Or, in our post-Roe context in states that allow abortions in cases of rape or incest, women have to recount these traumas to medical professionals that they have just met. Trans people have to recount a life where they've always known they were trans and cannot express or discuss doubts with those providing them health care.[12]

Shere was not forced by the state to recount her life in a certain way. But her autobiography was not exactly spontaneous; she didn't write it out of an urge to express herself but to clear her name in response to right-wing attacks of the 1980s and 1990s. If you tune your ear to her memoir in this way, you can hear the voices of her critics snarling, circling, and snapping at Shere's high heels on every page. They accuse her of being unhinged, deranged, crazy, and a liar, so she uses this book as a way to vindicate herself. The book denies anything bad ever happening in her life before *The Hite Report*. Perhaps she felt recounting those events would only subject her to more attacks. But this means her memoir offers no explanation as to why Shere wrote *The Hite Report*, nor does it depict her experience of four very distinct sexual cultures, which taught her that in all different ways, sex was a site of power, highly political and worthy of interrogation. For women to be free, sex had to change. This was what Shere Hite knew.

CHAPTER 2
BIG FEELINGS

In 1973, a woman from Long Island picked up Shere's questionnaire at a NOW meeting. She placed it carefully in her bag and, when she got home, filled it out in her neat cursive with a blue pen. She told Shere she was a Black woman and worked as an administrator. She had been raised in New York in a 'lower income' family, by a factory worker mother and an attorney father. Though she now identified as a lesbian and found relating sexually to women satisfying, she wrote of previous relationships with men. She described the way straight sex had gone through a numbered list: '1. kissing, 2. feeling the vagina, 3. sucking nipples, 4. oral sex, 5. penetration—How boring!!!' What she described was reflected in thousands of other women's responses. Secretaries aged thirty, mothers of four, older women who had been widowed for twenty years, almost all of them answered Shere's question 'How have most men had sex with you?' in this way. Across the board, sex consisted of a similar routine of foreplay, vaginal penetration and intercourse without clitoral stimulation, ending with male orgasm, which most men and women thought of as 'the natural end of sex'. No one asked these women how they felt, whether they found this kind of sex satisfying or what they might like instead. This was not because the men these women slept with were especially callous or cruel, but because of a false belief that what pleased men would also please women. 'Experts'—Freudian psychoanalysts, doctors, and sexologists as well as male lovers and husbands—told women that if they didn't find having sex like this pleasurable, or have orgasms frequently, the problem lay with them, and they needed help. This woman from Long Island had read lots of books about sex, she'd read Masters and Johnson and she'd read *The Joy of Sex*. She found them 'repetitious'. She hoped that Shere's book would be different and 'not run of the mill'.

Shere did do something new: She brought in the feelings. Across fifty-eight questions, she asked women, 'Is sex important to you?' and 'Do you enjoy masturbation? Physically? Psychologically?' It is hard to imagine a time when we didn't use personal experience to determine whether sex was good or bad and follow our feelings to make choices in sex. But this is a recent development, and we're in debt to Shere. *The Hite Report* was the first book in the English-speaking world to ask women how they felt about sex. But unlike much feminist talk about sex today, which suggests sharing feelings is enough to equalise sex, Shere knew that gendered power could not be so easily discarded. Sure, women could make immediate change, demand pleasure, and do it themselves, but Shere always insisted that for sex to be *really* great, society would have to be remade. This required feminism.

Shere learnt that women's feelings were a form of expertise from the women's movement, particularly from consciousness raising (CR). This is often described as *the* tactic of women's liberation, and tens of thousands of women were involved across the United States.[1] If women were already in the feminist movement, they would have seen notices for CR on the board at their local women's centre. Among the posters advertising campaigns for equal pay and self-defence classes, as well as leaflets encouraging women to help out at the local women's shelter or lay up the newsletter, there would have been announcements about CR groups. 'Sister', a typewritten notice might read, 'come and talk. Our consciousness-raising group needs new women. Join us, change every aspect of your life'. If women were not in the movement, CR was often a way in. Perhaps a friend, a cool aunt, or a fed-up colleague told them that there was a place where women—just women—could go and talk about how they felt and about how life actually was. The photos of CR groups show women sitting round, often on the floor (were there no chairs in the seventies?). Sometimes they hold wineglasses and cigarettes and the photo is clouded with smoke. Or they sit on a bed in a college dorm in a row, knees touching. CR took place in the suburbs too. I know of one group that met in the back room of a hair salon, a space for feminism alongside the boxes of curling lotion and shampoo. Wherever they are, in the photos, the women are animated, gesticulating, pointing, laughing, listening intently, leaning forward toward the speaker. Sometimes there is a seventies-style snack to eat, like carrot sticks dipped in cottage cheese, or cheese and pineapple on a cocktail stick with a red cellophane frill, or a pot of vegetable stew.

Most women are white in these photos, but not all.[2] CR was also indebted to politics and theory from what was then called the Third World, particularly Maoism. The influential New York–based feminist group Redstockings quoted Mao Zedong in their guide to consciousness raising.[3] On the wall of their office hung a poster encouraging women to learn from the Chinese Revolution and to 'Speak pains to recall pains', as well as the feminist reinterpretation to 'bitch sisters bitch'.

CR sessions were often based around 'questions of the night', which placed feelings front and centre. Women would take it in turns to answer questions like 'How do you feel about housework?' 'How do you feel about makeup and aging?'[4] At these groups, women talked openly and for the first time about feelings and experiences in all manner of things, including work, home, and relationships. CR was life-changing because women were able to put into words things they had never spoken about, contouring and colouring the silences that rained greyly through their lives. Many women discussed what they had done with their feelings of discontent. Until then, they had seen them as a personal deficiency and so had gone to psychoanalysis or the doctor. They had taken tranquilisers, or pretended they didn't feel so bad, but nothing seemed to work. At CR, women understood their feelings were political, the result of a deeply unequal world, not an individual failure. Women describe this moment of realisation as a 'click'. The Australian writer Helen Garner put it this way: 'I felt as if I'd been underwater my whole life. And now, for the first time I'd stuck my head out of the water and taken a breath, looking around and thinking "Now I get it. Now I get why my life is such a mess."'[5] Women could follow their feelings to find out what needed to be changed politically. Feelings became a form of expertise. This was the insight that Shere wanted to take from CR to *The Hite Report*. She wanted the book to be 'like a giant "rap session" on paper', as CR was sometimes called.

Shere came to CR in the most extraordinary way. While working unhappily as a model, sometimes in fashion, sometimes in porn, she did a job for the typewriter company Olivetti. At the shoot, the photographer told her to 'flirt with the camera and cross [her] legs provocatively', which left her feeling bad, even worse than she usually did after work. Soon after, Shere read that NOW had protested Olivetti over the very advertisement she had modelled for because it had a particularly sexist caption: 'The typewriter is so smart that she doesn't have to be'. Their placards read: 'Don't drown in an Olivetti typing pool'.

NOW was established in 1966. Founding members included Jewish feminist Betty Friedan, author of *The Feminine Mystique*, and Pauli Murray, the Black civil rights lawyer. NOW focussed on legal reform and political equality for women. As the organization was first based in Washington, DC, early members often worked within government departments, but they knew that to achieve equality their organisation would have to pressure the government from the outside too. NOW grew fast, went nationwide, and became the biggest women's rights organisation in the United States.[6]

Shere went alone to NOW. She felt nervous and wondered, 'Would they hate me?' She didn't want to be recognised as the Olivetti girl, so she wore no makeup. Halfway through, she got up the courage to whisper to the woman sitting next to her that she was the model in the advertisement. The woman announced this to the group, who welcomed her, saying, 'You see! Even the women in the ads don't like them'. Shere was hooked. She went alone to CR, and she too had her click, describing it as 'like a light suddenly switched on in a dark room'. In the women's movement she found what she had been looking for at grad school, 'the conversations we had in the movement, and the esprit de corps was wildly intoxicating. The movement's intellectual debates made Columbia look very pale and anaemic'. Particularly, she found matriarchy feminism inspiring and devoured theorists including theologian Mary Daly, archaeologist Marija Gimbutas, and writer Elizabeth Gould Davis. These feminists interpreted prehistoric evidence as proof of a matriarchal past, when women led peaceful and plentiful societies and when goddesses were worshipped. Inspired by this, Shere participated in a protest at the

Natural History Museum. The protestors disputed the way its displays and dioramas represented gender roles in ancient societies in exactly the same way as the present. Shere theorised, 'sexuality has not always been defined as we define it'. She thought there had been times in the distant past that were more liberatory for women. Matriarchy feminism certainly leant essentialist, but it appealed to many women for the way it understood patriarchy as a relatively recent phenomenon, which suggested that change was possible.[7] This may have appealed to Shere specifically because of her experience of both oppressive fundamentalist Christianity and sexist history at Columbia.

Shere also noticed something at CR that would inspire *The Hite Report* and so change her life. Women didn't talk about their own experiences and feelings about sex. The movement worked on campaigns for equal pay, abortion, and childcare—the latter two both consequences of sex—and talked about their feelings when it came to every other aspect of patriarchy, but sex was still considered private. Shere's life before the women's movement had taught her that sex was key to understanding how sexism functioned, how it structured the world and relations between men and women. Shere thought women should share how they actually had sex and their feelings about it. More than this, women must push through the collective vagaries about sex to redefine it for themselves, to move toward a new female sexuality. Redstockings feminist Anne Koedt had published her essay 'The Myth of the Vaginal Orgasm' in 1968 in which she argued forcefully that all orgasms were clitoral.[8] But Shere wondered if it were true. Shere suggested a weekend CR conference where sex was discussed frankly. The women were horrified: '"You think I'm going to stand up and tell everybody about how I have orgasms?! You've got to be kidding!"'

To get around women's embarrassment, Shere developed the anonymous questionnaire. She hand-printed the survey at the twenty-four-hour gay anarchist printing press and commune Come!Unity Press in the East Village. There was no door on the bathroom (privacy was bourgeois!), but there was a large risograph, which movement people could use if they provided their own ink. The Black Panthers printed material to demand the release of Assata Shakur, and New York Radical Women produced their CR guide there. There is a picture of Shere in the archive printing the questionnaires; she is feeding red ink, which matches her nails, into the printer. Her hair is pulled back and her silk scarf is tucked into her wool jumper to stop it dangling over the machine as she cranks the handle. She looks happy and purposeful. She printed the questionnaire in rainbow ink on pastel-coloured scrap paper and offcuts of old Bingo cards, which she bought cheaply. Shere decorated the questionnaires with love hearts, cupid bows and arrows, and starbursts. She received compliments for this: 'Think the paper and variegated type is beautiful'. The aesthetic resembles a teenage diary, not a clinical questionnaire, a choice Shere likely made to disarm the recipient, and to encourage honesty and confessional responses. She received an abundance of these. One woman wrote to her: 'I've kept a journal for fourteen years without ever being able to write this candidly about my sex life. I was able to let out hidden things I'd otherwise never tell a soul'.

Feminists in NOW weren't totally convinced of Shere's sex project. Working on other campaigns, they didn't see sex as that important to women's liberation. Regina Ryan, Shere's editor, told me when we spoke that NOW 'thought [Shere] a fringey character'. They 'disdained her a little bit, disregarded her, wrote her off. They didn't think much of her work'. Martin Sage, Shere's then-boyfriend, explained that her focus on sex was seen as 'less serious, less political, less meaningful than their attempts at organising or legislating that could be put on paper as opposed to only be understood in a bedroom'. Muriel Fox, then president of NOW, called the questionnaire 'self-selecting'. Fox reflected on this apologetically in her recent memoir: 'Her questionnaire did not receive the enthusiastic response it deserved. We failed to realize the important knowledge Shere would contribute to world understanding of women's sexual needs'.[9] At the time, Shere was hurt. But NOW still agreed to let her use their logo and address, which she printed on the front. Without NOW's brand, the survey would not have spread so widely. Without the broader women's movement, it would have had nowhere to go. If she had started the project even five years earlier, in the late 1960s, there would have been hardly any feminist bookshops or health centres and very few feminist magazines and newsletters where she could send her surveys. NOW helped her get beyond the radical women's movement, because their networks extended to suburban women, working women, even Republicans. Shere wanted the survey to go further still and sent seventy-five thousand copies through abortion rights groups and church newsletters. The questionnaire was also reproduced by *Brides* and *Mademoiselle*. *Oui*, a porn mag 'for the man of the world', ran it 'in the interest of better communication [with] women'. It appeared alongside a centrefold of 'better girls than last month'. Men passed it to their wives and girlfriends. Women who came across the questionnaire showed it wide-eyed to their female friends, the women in their family, the students they taught.

WHILE NOW AND SHERE DIDN'T see eye to eye, other feminists were very supportive. Barbara Seaman, the feminist health activist and author of *Free and Female*, loved the project. She told Regina Ryan, then working at Knopf, about Shere. As Seaman described Shere, Ryan realised she had seen her around the neighbourhood. They lived right across the street from each other: 'She walked this little dog. She always looked so glamorous, she had hair like Lucille Ball, strawberry blonde, piled on top of her head . . . I couldn't believe that's who it was'. Ryan wrote to Shere, inviting her to lunch at her favourite French restaurant near Knopf, eager to hear more about her idea. The meeting was 'an extraordinary event'. Shere walked in, 'she had this great white lacy tiered dress on . . . Her look was a shepherdess from a French eighteenth-century opera, not a real shepherdess, but a beautiful shepherdess, singing'. Shere was 'so gorgeous' that as she walked in, everything in the restaurant 'kind of stopped'. She sat down and started 'telling me about the book and her work. She had a very high-pitched voice and she was singing out things like "vulva" and "orgasm." I just said, "oh yes, isn't that interesting." The whole restaurant was like "what's going on over there!" It was quite a moment. I was so impressed by her, she had done such a lot of work, and thinking. I was just blown away by her. No one had ever asked women what they wanted, what they felt, what they enjoyed. So, every woman in the world was going to want to read this. It was liberating and so new. So I signed it up'.

Ryan took the book with her when she moved from Knopf to Macmillan as the first female editor-in-chief of a U.S. publishing house. Shere wanted to call the book *Diana Rising*, a nod to the goddess and hunter Diana, who was heralded in the matriarchy feminism Shere found so inspiring. She signed the contract with that title. It was Ryan who suggested calling it *The Hite Report*. She told me her husband had come up with it: 'He said, "That's easy. *The Kinsey Report* just came out. This is "The Hite Report." He was a very clever titler, he did it with a finger snap . . . It was perfect'. It is doubtful that if they had gone with *Diana Rising*, the book would have been the success it was. It is also doubtful that it would have been so fully entangled with Shere, to the extent that she was the book and the book was her. This became complicated when her work was vilified in the 1980s, because there was no space between her and what she produced. When her work was attacked viciously, so was she.

Shere's advance from Macmillan was $20,000. She made it work. Her basement apartment opposite Ryan's was rent controlled and cheap at $450 per month. Ryan described it as 'funky, fun, and full of odd furniture'. Shere decorated with throw pillows, beaded lampshades, beautiful fabrics. She didn't go out much, working vampire hours through the night because she was so dedicated to, even obsessed by, the project. Her beloved dog Rusty was her primary companion. She lived cheaply on devilled eggs. Sometimes Ryan would visit the apartment to offer edits and help Shere with the book. Ryan stressed how good she was to work with, how smart, driven, and charming. She was also so gorgeous: 'I mean, it really was a distraction. I'd look at her and think, "This woman is so beautiful." I'd have to shake my head and get back to work'.

The project was huge, and Shere employed two assistants, Dylan Landis and Veronica Di Napoli, who worked hard to find patterns in the raw material of surveys and turn them into statistics. Landis had met Shere at a NOW conference. She described the meeting evocatively when we spoke: 'I wandered the hall and came to a card table with this stunning woman behind it and all these questionnaires on brown paper . . . and they were all about sex, which no one had ever spoken to me frankly about. I said to her, "What is this?" She said, "I'm writing a book, and this is for my research. Take one"'. Landis had 'never met anybody doing something so interesting, and [she] wanted to latch onto it', so she boldly said: 'I want to work for you. Can I work for you for free?' Landis visited Shere's apartment once or twice a week to help with the book. Shere found the money to pay her $2 an hour, not much, but it was much needed. After her classes finished at Barnard, Landis would take the bus to Shere's. Shere would hand her giant sheets of graph paper with a question written across the top, like 'Do you like to masturbate with your knees up or down, legs open or closed?' Landis would work in the carpeted hallway, just outside Shere's front door, so she could chain-smoke. She was quite flexible, so she would sit cross-legged or with her legs outstretched, leaning over the graph paper and tabulate for a few hours, ashing into a saucer and tallying up the responses. The work enthralled her; it chimed with Landis's interest in psychology, and she sensed it might become important. A testimony like 'I lie on my stomach and he's on my back reaching up under me and makes me come and come and come and he won't stop and he won't let up. Wow!' became a tally mark in the column labelled 'clit. stim'. Landis recalled: 'I had to find the correct place for those answers. That was my job, to put the mark in the column. If I got that wrong, the statistics would be wrong'. Then Shere would make her a hamburger, frying the patty in her little kitchen. Sometimes if Shere had read something that intrigued her in a questionnaire, she would send Landis with homework, urging her to try a new position with her boyfriend. Landis avoided this because, like so many women at the time, she 'didn't know how to communicate about sex'. Once, she had tried. She told a lover he should touch her 'a little higher up' and he had snapped back 'What are you, a policewoman?' She never asked again.

Shere taught Landis that writing a book was possible, but working for her wasn't always straightforward. As others have confirmed, Shere was very sensitive and quick to take offence. Once she wanted to get into the library at Columbia and asked to borrow Landis's photo ID. Landis explained to me: 'I wasn't particularly pretty in college, I wasn't unpretty but I was very flat chested and skinny. My hair just kind of hung there. And Sherry was so beautiful, and looked like a movie star.

And I said, "Sherry, you don't look anything like me"'. And in 'a fully self-deprecating way', Landis added, "Don't you wish you did?" Shere became very angry. She said, '"I am so hurt that you would say that. That is such an insulting thing to say." I was speechless. All I could do was apologize'. Shere eventually 'moved past it', but it took a long time. After that, Landis felt she had to be careful: 'I was afraid I was going to put my foot in it in some way that I couldn't foresee'.

The Hite Report took years of work, and Shere ran out of her advance. She borrowed money from friends and got into $24,000 of debt. The book, she told the press, was 'financed by angels'. These angels included old boyfriends, and even Regina Ryan's doorman Virginio Del Toro. She got to know Del Toro on her breaks. Working through the night, she would leave her apartment at 2:00 or 3:00 a.m. to walk Rusty and stop for a chat with him. He asked why her light was on so late, so often. 'She told me she was working on the book. It sounded a very good idea and very important . . . She needed money, she was a good girl, a hard-working girl who never went to parties or anything, so I offered to help her'.

Most of the people who she borrowed money from were men. The press insinuated that this was because she slept around, but she explained it was because they 'have a lot easier time getting loans than women do'. At the time, women did not have easy access to credit. To get a loan, unmarried women needed a male relative to cosign, and husbands had to sign for their wives. It didn't matter that Shere had a $20,000 advance from Macmillan, as these conditions applied even in cases when women outearned men. If a married couple sought a loan, the woman's income didn't count toward the amount they could borrow, because banks thought that as soon as women fell pregnant, they would stop earning and stop contributing to repayments. To have women's income count, some couples took what were known as 'baby letters' from their doctors to the bank, which testified that she was on birth control or had a hysterectomy.[10] Feminists like Bella Abzug and women in NOW were focussed on access to credit in the early 1970s, and thanks to them, the Equal Credit Opportunity Act passed in 1974. But banks continued to discriminate. Pretty women and those who had lived for a long time on the economic margins—women like Shere—were denied loans by bank managers who thought them a credit risk because they assumed these women would be pregnant soon, too. So feminists did it themselves. Those who were critical of capitalism established credit unions like Sistershares in Massachusetts. To borrow money here, women had to be a member of a feminist group, and staff were happy to provide a list. The First Women's Bank in New York was a more mainstream, for-profit venture.[11] Shere opened an account with them after the success of *The Hite Report*, but these financial institutions came around a little late in the book process, so she relied on friends.

The final push necessary to get *The Hite Report* over the line was a rent strike. Shere's building was infested with rats, the hallway covered in pigeon droppings, and the boiler faulty, operating only sporadically across the winter. She wrote to her landlord, complaining, 'I am sitting here, I thought I would stay home and get some work done tonight, but how can I work when I am freezing?' He sent nasty letters in return, saying, 'instead of reading on "women's lib" and "tenants lib" exclusively, try a few on "landlords lib"— you might be unpleasantly shocked into reality'. Shere and her fellow tenants withheld rent and took the landlord to court. They were told they would have to leave eventually, but their eviction date was in six months' time, and until then they could stay rent free. This was how she finished the book.

AFTER YEARS OF COLLATING SURVEY responses, Shere reached her major conclusions: The majority of women were sexually dissatisfied, and only 30 percent of women could orgasm regularly from intercourse, that is, 'the penis thrusting in the vagina'. Women could easily orgasm from masturbation, which invariably involved clitoral stimulation, but sex rarely did. Many women described a sexual routine that was similar to the one this chapter opened with: 'A little kiss, a little feel, a finger for arousal, a touch of breast, and he's on top, wham it's over'. Invariably, male orgasm determined the end of sex. Women who had several, or many, lovers noted that this pattern was replicated among the majority of men they had slept with: 'I'm beginning to think there must be something like a sexual "Robert's Rules of Order" which every guy follows'. Whether women slept with sexual revolution radicals, hippies who strummed guitars and drank red wine and read *The Joy of Sex* with ecclesiastical fervour, or straitlaced husbands who caught the 8:03 a.m. to the city, the routine was the same, and they were unsatisfied.

Many women faked orgasms. Women told Shere how it felt to perform, to convince: 'For fifteen years I was the world's best faker. Honestly—they should [give me] a phallic trophy—mounted on a pedestal (like in the art history books)'. Sometimes women even taught themselves to simulate the physical feeling of orgasm: 'it's better for him to feel a contracting vagina, but you can also do that at will if you practice'. Women faked it so that sex could end: 'Several times I faked orgasm when I couldn't stand a heavy, hairy, rough body crushing me'. Another wrote, 'Yes . . . I have faked a number of times . . . I want him to have his orgasm so I can go to sleep'. But why was this? Where did this routine come from? Why was it so common? Why didn't women speak up about it?

IN THEIR SURVEYS, MANY WOMEN explained they learnt the correct and 'normal' way to have sex from Freud. Shere described him as the 'founding father of the vaginal orgasm', and *The Hite Report* shows how pervasive his theories were. In his *Three Essays on the Theory of Sexuality*, published in 1905, Freud grafted ideas of *immature/mature* and *healthy/dysfunctional* forms of female sexuality onto the vagina and clitoris, respectively. According to Freud, girls find pleasure in their clitoris, just as young boys do in their penis, but as girls mature into women, so the pleasure centre moves from the clitoris to the vagina as women 'put aside their childish masculinity'. In the mature, heterosexual woman, Freud located the erotic and the reproductive in the same place, the vagina. Freud was writing in the late nineteenth and early twentieth century, a time when the clitoris was largely superfluous and the purpose of sex for women was considered to be entirely reproductive and for the pleasure of men. At this time, textbooks such as the 'doctors' bible', *Gray's Anatomy*, did not label or discuss the function of the clitoris.[12] According to Freud, the clitoris would naturally 'transmit excitation to the adjacent sexual parts' the way a 'pine shaving' would help 'set a log of harder wood on fire'. The 'log' he is referring to is the vagina, but this simile choice is a monstrous Freudian slip; he rather gives himself away exposing who the vaginal orgasm was for, and whose pleasure it would increase. If grown women could not orgasm vaginally because the 'vaginal orifice remained 'anaesthet[ised]', this was because of their sexual immaturity.[13] This should be treated with psychoanalysis. In other words, not being able to orgasm vaginally was a mental illness.[14]

One woman wrote: 'It would give me a great deal of personal pleasure to give Freud a black eye', and Shere suggested that 'probably millions of women could agree'. The problem was not Freud so much as his conservative neo-Freudian followers. Freud, after all, had made pathbreaking discoveries. Like feminists, he understood the family as crucial to the formation of the self. He also knew that inside us all was a roaring ocean, that we are split and divided against ourselves. This came up again and again in CR: Women wanted equality with men but acted against their own interests; women wanted a more pleasurable sex life but were afraid to ask for it, sometimes afraid to get it. Shere thought Freud would have accepted new directions in the field, but wrote, 'the profession he originated has been unwilling and slow to do so'. Many women who could not orgasm vaginally had been sent to Freudian psychotherapy, which wholly embraced anti-feminism from the 1940s onward. This reified the model of heterosexual sex based on male pleasure and reproduction as the most satisfying, indeed the only, model for 'mature' feminine women. In therapy, women were told that their lack of vaginal orgasm was a result of neurotic blocks and deficiencies in the psyche, and they believed it: 'I can have an orgasm with clitoral stimulation but I have never had one with intercourse. This is purely a fear thing . . . My therapist helped me see it'. Another woman spoke of how she came to see clitoral orgasm as 'selfish and infantile (thanks to Freud, I guess)', so she no longer expected to orgasm in intercourse.

Conservative neo-Freudians told women their inability to orgasm vaginally was a symptom of their refusal to adjust to their role as women. Women couldn't come purely from penetration because they refused their passive, maternal place in the bedroom and the family. Shere suggested that 'even if women were not in analysis themselves the influence of these psychiatric theories on women has been strong and pervasive . . . endlessly repeated—from women's magazines, popular psychologists and men during sex', and in manuals on child raising and marriage, films, and novels. Freudian Helen Deutsch's *The Psychology of Women* was in its eleventh reprint by 1960, and many women mentioned they had read it. In this book, Deutsch suggested that in the case of new brides, the vagina would have to be brought into feeling and turned into an erogenous zone, 'overpowered' by 'man's aggressive penetration'. This wasn't sexual assault, but women's 'latent readiness' being enabled.[15] If this sounds like someone saying rape is actually sex and women *know they want it* deep down, that's because it is.

In their surveys, women used therapeutic language to scold themselves for their lack of vaginal orgasm; one woman wrote, 'I must learn to let go, relax and trust, unlearn my taboos and defences'. In other words, they blamed themselves. This is why feminists like Shere, Shulamith Firestone, and Betty Friedan critiqued psychoanalysis. As they saw it, psychoanalysis blamed women for their own bad feelings, when in fact they were political, evidence of an oppressive social role. Therapy helped women to accept the unacceptable, like roles based on sexism and on racism. Psychoanalysis was not a place where women could air their difficult feelings around sex without judgment, or question the importance of the vaginal orgasm, or self-actualise. It was a place where women learnt to adjust their feelings to the conditions around them. [16]

SHERE'S OWN EXPERIENCES OF ANALYSIS in the very early 1970s reflected this. She saw a Dr Boles for 'treatment'. At this time, she had a particularly bad boyfriend, Jesse. He was misogynistic and physically violent, and she was unable to relax around him because of his 'tyrannical persecution'. She felt she should be tasting glitter in her mouth, but marvellous New York was crushingly lonely most of the time. She wrote: 'Giving my nude body and rested face' over 'for bad pictures . . . What an ugly city. The noise and vulturism is about to kill me, and I have no one to talk to'. She had no female friends, and sought approval in men, though she found them 'mediocre'. They saw her as 'beautiful and desirable' but also as 'an item for consumption . . . used by many men and thrown away, like garbage'. She was aware of this pattern but couldn't seem to get on top of it. She was occasionally suicidal.

Dr Boles suggested that Shere's violent relationship and attraction to unsuitable men was because her father abandoned her just after she was born. Her therapist framed her problem as neediness and attention-seeking developed in childhood. She noted: 'I pick old patterned relationships bec. I don't think enough of myself for new ones'. But Dr Boles never discussed sexism or the rigid gender roles in her family. He never considered poverty, or how having no money made it more difficult to extract yourself from bad relationships. Shere wrote of their 'disagreements as to women's and my place'. Boles framed his perspective as 'realism'. Shere saw him as a 'chauvinist', clipping her wings. After she finished treatment, he left a strange 'gift' outside her door, a furry mechanical dog. It reminded Shere 'of the presents a father gives his small daughter' to reinforce 'the super sweet bond which girls supposedly enjoy'. She summed it up: 'I certainly didn't feel like I was being treated much like a person'. No doubt drawing on her experience of psychoanalysis, along with thousands of other women's testimonies, Shere wrote: 'I wish we could have back all the time and energy we have spent blaming ourselves . . . And all the money we spent [on] psychiatrists . . . I would like to have [seen] what we would have built with that energy'.

SHERE WAS CURIOUS ABOUT WHERE else women had learnt about sex, besides Freud. In her questionnaire, she asked about sexology: 'Have you read Masters and Johnson's recent scientific studies on human sexual response . . . ? What did you think of them? Of Kinsey? Any other writers?' Did this newer work help women flip the sexual script? Working from 1938 until his death in 1956, Kinsey was interested in sexual *behaviour*, not how people felt about the sex they were having. Through in-depth interviews with eighteen thousand people, he sought to learn how people had sex and measure the frequency of sexual activities. Beyond the binary model of *healthy/dysfunctional, mature/immature, deviant/acceptable* favoured by neo-Freudians, Kinsey came up with a scale. He aimed to find out what types of behaviour were most common, irrespective of what social norms dictated people *should* be doing.[17] He fearlessly asked: Did people have sex outside marriage? With people of the same sex, in public, or with animals? As Shere explained on *The Mike Douglas Show*, 'Kinsey did a service in putting on the map how often people did what with whom. My area was a little different, I asked people why do you do it, how do you feel about it. Would you like things to be different? I'm really trying to draw a larger picture of society and how people are feeling within that society'. Kinsey found that women could orgasm from intercourse, but for many women this was inconsistent. Of those women who were orgasming, Kinsey did not enquire whether clitoral stimulation was involved. Shere thought this was key.

Masters and Johnson were interested in how people responded physically and anatomically to sex. They conducted direct laboratory observation of nearly ten thousand sex acts between the late 1950s up until 1965. They hooked up volunteers—initially sex workers—to wires, which enabled them to measure heart rate during sex and contractions during orgasm. They observed women having sex with a glass dildo called Ulysses (yes, really!). The light and camera within Ulysses allowed them to see inside the vagina during sex, and observe the moment of orgasm.[18] This led to the conclusion, important for *The Hite Report*, that all women's orgasms were clitoral orgasms, and that women who were orgasming from intercourse were doing so because the clitoris was indirectly stimulated by the penis. Feminist Anne Koedt relied on this new sexology, suggesting that Kinsey and Masters and Johnson made it clear that there was no such thing as a vaginal orgasm. Masters and Johnson could have staged a coup. They could have deposed penetration as the highest form of sex, and instead discussed masturbation, clitoral stimulation, and lesbian sex as possibilities. Alas, they did not. Instead, they suggested most women could orgasm from the indirect stimulation of the clitoris during penetration, that this was automatic, part of the 'normal' course of sex. Shere described Masters and Johnson's theory as a 'Rube-Goldberg model', a chain-reaction machine that completes a simple task in a comedic, overcomplicated way. Sure, she said, some women do orgasm from this kind of secondary stimulation, if their lover doesn't come too quickly, if it works for her to be on top, if their bodies fit together perfectly like two puzzle pieces, but there was a much easier way. Denying clitoral stimulation was like suggesting that men should be able to orgasm from having their testicles touched, which might indirectly stimulate the penis and eventually cause orgasm. 'Women', Shere wrote wryly, 'would have to be patient and "understand"' if this indirect form of stimulation 'did not lead to orgasm "every time"' for their male lovers.

Shere concluded that Masters and Johnson never suggested direct clitoral stimulation for women because 'they continued to view sex through certain cultural blinders'. Shere is being a little too diplomatic here; these two were deeply committed to monogamous, heterosexual marriage as the highest form of relationship. From 1968 they ran a treatment program for 'dissatisfied homosexual men' helping them to 'convert' to heterosexuality, which continued long after homosexuality was repealed as a psychological disorder and long after the advent of gay liberation. Masters and Johnson's ideas about women reflected these values too. Their theories meant there was no need for men to have sex differently and maintained the predictable sex that so many women found unsatisfying.

Masters and Johnson's and Kinsey's research projects were works of sexual science. They used up-to-date scientific methods to generate their findings. Kinsey used an early IBM computer, and Masters and Johnson worked in the lab, very different from Dylan Landis tabulating in Shere's hallway. The scientific approach bled into the writing; while the turgid prose gave these sexologists an air of expertise, the most liberating findings were often submerged, and women reported finding 'these men in white coats' hard to grasp. Masters and Johnson describe orgasm as 'those few seconds during which the vasoconcentration and myotonia developed from sexual stimuli are released'.[19] With descriptions like that, *Human Sexual Response* was 'the most purchased, least read book in America', as Masters himself put it.[20] Kinsey's finding about the importance of the clitoris appears on page 592 of a book that stretches over 800 pages—way to bury the lede! By keeping women's feelings front and centre, the descriptions of orgasms in *The Hite Report* are incomparable to how orgasms were rendered in earlier sexology. There is no 'vasoconcentration' here, but 'It's a peak of almost, almost, ALMOST, ALMOSTTT. The only way I can describe it is to say it's like riding the "Tilt-a-Whirl"'.

To shake up the orthodoxies of sexual science, Shere wrote to Martin Sage, the editor of *Sexology,* a well-respected, widely distributed magazine, to ask if she might share her findings. She wrote a letter by hand in red felt pen on frosted green paper. This was unusual, as all the queries Sage received were typewritten. 'It was lovely handwriting, lots of lovely flourishes', he told me. He kept shuffling it to the top of his inbox. They met for lunch, and Sage realised that she was 'writing not simply from a physiological, sexological point of view but from a political point of view', quite different from the approach of *Sexology* at that time. She rolled her eyes when Sage mentioned Masters and Johnson. They spent hours talking, and it was clear that there was mutual attraction. Sage called his office to let them know he would be late, and Shere 'crawled into the phone booth with him'. By the time he had got back to the office, she had called three times. They began a relationship that would last three years. It was not always easy, but it was always interesting, full of 'unreproducible moments, because there was no one like her. And anyone who'd ever met her would agree'.

SHERE'S PURSUIT OF SAGE INDICATES a rebellion against rigid and repressive sexual norms that shook the United States in the late 1960s, known as the sexual revolution. Shere asked women about that too. Women reported that they were pleased about the new culture of openness, the way the contraceptive pill made it possible for them to have sex without worrying about pregnancy. People explored different ways of living and loving, including with multiple partners, where children were raised by many parents rather than in a nuclear family. Censorship decreased, films began to include sex and nudity, and books celebrating sex were published. Women told Shere they had read Nancy Friday's *My Secret Garden* and Erica Jong's novel *Fear of Flying*, both published three years before *The Hite Report*, and blockbusters too. Both brought to light women's sexual fantasies. The sexual revolution declared sex healthy and necessary, and many women liked that.

Women also read Alex Comfort's illustrated guide to sex for couples, *The Joy of Sex*, first published in 1972, the title a play on *The Joy of Cooking*. Comfort encouraged readers to consider sex the way they would gastronomic arts: Couples might come to grips with the basics, grouped under 'starters', and were encouraged to experiment with some 'sauces and pickles' as they worked toward chef de cuisine status and mastered the mains. The drawings are very seventies, and there is so much hair in this book. She has hairy underarms, he has a large handlebar moustache, and everyone has voluminous, curling pubes. They make love on a bed that puts Tracey Emin's to shame. There is some breathtakingly casual racism throughout, with positions named for particular countries, for example 'Japanese-style' and 'Indian-style', and in this it resembles the cookbooks of the 1970s in another way: Orientalism is at the fore. Plus, all the snacks and appetisers are really just foreplay. Even Comfort can't get away from the routine; the end is still penis-in-vagina sex: 'the main dish is loving, unselfconscious intercourse . . . good old face-to-face matrimonial'.[21] The clitoris is given only four sentences across the volume, while the penis is discussed and drawn over and over. A Black lesbian who filled out Shere's survey remarked that she 'didn't think much' of *The Joy of Sex*.

The openness and enthusiasm of the sexual revolution were not enough to change women's sex lives. More sex didn't mean better sex; men still expected women to have sex with them their way, in a way that maximised male pleasure. Shere explained that when women did challenge this, taking the bricks out of the wall of silence and speaking through the gaps, their partners often filled them in again just as quickly. One woman asked for clitoral stimulation, and her husband said, 'Only whores enjoy clitoral contact and going down on a man', so she gave up asking. Another woman asked her lovers to 'stimulate [her] manually' and 'they became insulting and suggested I've had lesbian experiences'. Women also felt they had 'lost their right to say "no"'. As one woman wrote drily, 'Sure women are liberated, liberated to get laid'. Another described how 'Most men didn't give a damn about whether I wanted to have sex with them or not: If I didn't want to screw them, they'd . . . try to lecture me into being "free"'. Sexual inequality percolated through the sexual revolution, and when sexual freedom was discussed, there was almost always a silent 'for men' on the end.

Women didn't speak up about how they felt or what they wanted because the stakes were too high materially, something I am sure Shere could relate to. In response to the question 'Do you think that sex is in any way political?' women talked about how sex and economics were linked. One middle-class woman explained, 'In my circle generally the man makes twice as much money as the wife. That means if you like your lifestyle—your swimming pool, shrink, dishwasher, neighbourhood—you don't chuck it all to run off with some surfer'. Older women who had been married for decades before the women's movement and young women who had grown up in conservative households talked about how they used sex to barter 'for a new sofa or a night out' or to appease a husband who 'pays for everything'. A woman who experienced real hardship talked about times when she would say yes to a dinner date, 'just for the chance to eat something besides spaghetti'. She knew these men usually wanted sex, and 'the less I was able to afford the dinner he was paying for, the more I felt I owed it to him'.

Shere called this 'sexual slavery'. She explained: 'Women are sexual slaves insofar as they are (justifiably) afraid to "come out" with their own sexuality, and forced to satisfy others' needs and ignore their own'. Certainly, what Shere described is oppressive, but it is very different from *actual* slavery, where people are reduced to things, their humanity stripped from them across their lives, in every moment. It also ignores the history of women who were actually *sexually enslaved*. The woman-as-slave metaphor has a long history and is a crude analogy of gendered and racial oppression favoured by white feminists.[22] Early editions of *Ms.* magazine feature many images of women in bridal garb, their ankles weighted down with the ball and chain of chattel slavery. This comparison was used by other feminists who also discussed sex, which Shere drew on. In 'Vaginal Orgasm as Mass Hysterical Survival Response', Ti-Grace Atkinson freely deploys the N-word and likens the woman who had 'learnt' to orgasm vaginally to the enslaved person who had 'learnt to shuffle', that is, coerced to dance and perform happiness for their master, a metaphor that is reused by Anne Koedt.[23]

It is likely that Shere and other feminists relied on this analogy because both Black and white men on the left at this time did not take feminism as seriously as they took the war in Vietnam and civil rights.[24] But Shere's use of sexual slavery revealed the book's limits, and white feminists' racism and ignorance of Black women's experience of *actual* enslavement, including its essential sexual dimensions. As Angela Davis wrote, 'Slavery relied as much on routine sexual abuse as it relied on the whip and the lash'. These conditions of enslavement gave birth to the potent myth where sexual assaults against Black women by white men were 'ideologically sanctioned' and Black women were seen as naturally 'promiscuous and immoral'. This myth was necessary because Black women provided the labour force for slavery, through birthing children and by expressing slaveowners' total ownership of Black people. It survived well beyond the abolition of slavery, naturalising the act of rape against Black women and stripping Black women of their right to say no in the eyes of both perpetrators and the state.

The inseparable companion to the myth of the promiscuous Black woman was, as Davis argued, the 'Black man as sexual monster'. False rape accusations were used by white men and women to frame Black men as part of racist terror in the Jim Crow era. This resulted in a campaign of white violence and lynching against Black men. [25] As scholars make clear, these twin myths of Black sexuality continued to determine the sex lives of Black women and made it difficult for Black women to speak out against male violence. If the perpetrator was white, Black women were often disbelieved because of their alleged promiscuity; if the perpetrator was Black, they were told they were acting as a mouthpiece for white supremacy, siding against Black men and perpetuating the myth of him as a rapist.[26] These powerful narratives, which entwined sexuality with race, affected the lives of Black women and the kind of sex they were having, at least as much as Freudian psychoanalysis and sexology did, but unlike these other narratives, this goes undiscussed in *The Hite Report*. Shere lacked Black feminist and intersectional analysis. Due to the ongoing intellectual efforts and political work of feminists of colour, this is more well integrated into feminism today.

But we still have much to learn from Shere. For women to change their sex lives, she recommended that they take the insights of feminism into the bedroom. Women might stop flocking to psychiatrists in search of their 'vaginal destiny' and 'stop waiting' in sex for 'men to "mete out the goodies"'. For women to get what they wanted, they should challenge the rigidities of sex that prioritised male pleasure and ended with his orgasm, 'do it [yourself], whatever it is—or ask for it, very clearly and very specifically . . . care about yourself, please yourself, feel it is your right'. In these moments, *The Hite Report* resembles contemporary liberal feminist guides to sex. In a very upbeat register, these suggest we might talk about our feelings and desires before, during, and after sex, and happy orgasmic sex will surely follow.[27] But there is a difference between today's liberal feminism and the feminism Shere advocated for in *The Hite Report*. Liberal feminism suggests gendered inequality can be overcome in sex, by talking about feelings and prioritizing choices, all of which are valid, and which both people can equally express. Shere suggested this was not a bad start, but she knew that structural inequality couldn't really be solved by a woman and a man during sex, no matter how honest and feelings-forward they were. This was because inequality pervades our choices and feelings, and shapes our desires, long before we've even set foot in the bedroom. Shere wanted to 'redefine sex and physical relations as we know them', and to do this, something more radical was required.

Shere suggested that heterosexual women might look to lesbians, who she said had begun to liberate sex. These women provided a stark contrast to the often-discontented straight women in the book. The sexual scripts and rigid routine that weighed so heavily on heterosexual couples were not inscribed here. One woman wrote joyfully, 'The first woman I was in love with (when I was twelve) had a smell like wild woods and autumn leaves and I loved it. I like to smell my lover's hair and breasts and her melt. I like to suck her breasts and I like her to suck mine. I've never felt like I do with her. I like the little things she does better than all the orgasms in the world'. Women often remarked on how thoughtful their female lovers were: 'My lover is very sensitive to what I want . . . the other night when she was being gentle and I wasn't responding much . . . I said "I want you to be rough" and so she was and it was strong and wonderful'. In *The Hite Report*, lesbian sex is allowed to be awkward, funny, silly and real. One woman remarked that while her lover was 'always emotionally involved . . . [s]ometimes her mind wanders, like once we were starting to make love and all of a sudden, she says "What part of the world do armadillos live in?" Really, she was serious, and we laughed a long time'.

INCLUDING LESBIANS IN *THE HITE Report* was radical. In the early moments of women's liberation, many lesbians felt they could not speak about their desire. Adrienne Rich had identified that 'compulsory heterosexuality'—the belief that everyone is heterosexual, or they ought to be—structured American culture.[28] It also structured the women's movement. In 1969, Betty Friedan, then president of NOW, warned of a 'lavender menace' (a play on the anti-communist 'red menace'): lesbians who threatened the respectability of the women's movement by trying to force it into alignment with lesbian rights.[29] Friedan later apologised. But at the time, lesbian feminists refused to hide in fear and keep silent; they called out the movement's homophobic paranoia. At a feminist conference in 1970, they wore hand-dyed purple T-shirts that read *Lavender Menace* and gave out a leaflet that read: 'Women in the movement are hostile, evasive, or try to incorporate [lesbianism] into some broader issue. But it is absolutely essential. As long as the label "dyke" can be used to frighten women into a less militant stand . . . [then] . . . she is controlled by the male culture . . . A lesbian is the rage of all women condensed to the point of explosion'.[30]

While the women's movement had changed by 1976, *The Hite Report* was always intended as a book for the world beyond, which was still stubbornly homophobic. Shere suggested that straight women should not blandly accept and tolerate lesbians but look to them as a model, a group of women who were not beholden to a sexual script based on male desire. As Shere wrote, 'there is no one institutionalized way of having [sex], so [lesbians] can be as inventive and individual as the people involved'. Shere saw lesbian sex as prefigurative for straight women, not in the sense that all women should become lesbians, but they should learn to have sex *like* lesbians. By the time *The Hite Report* was published, many feminists had abandoned heterosex as irredeemably sexist and were recommending lesbian separatism to straight women. Shere's vision was an antidote to this nihilism; she suggested it wasn't who you fucked but how.

As Shere saw it, though, women *should* become feminists. Changing the world beyond the bedroom into a more just and equal place would *really* expand sexual possibilities. In the long term, a gender-just world would remake the conditions that shaped desires and change the context that moulded choices. As one woman wrote, 'feminism is a bottomless entity to discover incredible treasures none of us may be aware of'. But Shere thought that in the present, too, feminist struggle would change women, including at the molecular level of desire; they would see other people and themselves differently. Shere gave space over to women who discussed how this social movement had changed their sex lives: 'With the onset of the women's movement and its personal effect on me, I've stopped faking.' Another wrote: 'I don't think I ever asked for what I wanted . . . Now the women's movement has helped me to be outspoken. I ask for what I want in all sorts of situations—church, work, the supermarket, local government—and in bed'. It was women's liberation that would make 'a new kind of physical relations to go with a new, more humane and pro-women society'. This was the feminist message of *The Hite Report*. In the next chapter we will see how Shere and her book travelled far beyond the women's movement, and how this message was received by hundreds of thousands of women.

CHAPTER 3
NORMAL WOMEN AND OTHERS

In May of 1977, a housewife and mother of five grown kids who was '40ish' and living in Levittown, Pennsylvania, an archetypal postwar suburb where each house and garden was identical to the next, sat down at her husband's typewriter while he was out working as a removalist. She rested her fingers on the keys, her nails freshly polished, wound the dial to feed the paper through, and began a letter to Shere Hite. She had seen Shere on her favourite talk show, *Phil Donahue*, discussing the major findings of *The Hite Report*. Hearing that sexual dissatisfaction among American women was widespread, that 70 percent of women could not orgasm from penetrative sex alone and required clitoral stimulation, and that most women could easily masturbate to orgasm, she felt 'a cloud of guilt and ignorance was completely lifted'.

She told Shere that across twenty-two years of marriage, 'my husband would quickly touch my clitoris and I'd pray "Please continue" but he never did and I was left unfulfilled and uptight. It got so bad I found myself refusing his advances and he accused me of being frigid . . . I had thought that something was wrong with me because the penis thrusting did nothing for me', but now she knew she was 'normal . . . Fortunately my husband was home the morning of your program and he was stunned. We both watched spellbound . . . He asked, "Is all that true?" I nodded my head yes. We proceeded to bed and experimented. For the first time in my life I experienced [a] gigantic orgasm with him . . . We spent half the day in bed. My husband and I are ecstatic . . . All our friends see us kissing, whispering and making private jokes to each other. You, Miss Hite, saved our marriage and made it a dream . . . Keep up the good work, we in the suburbs are all for it'. She sealed the letter. As she went to post it, she might have wondered if her neighbours had read *The Hite Report* or seen Shere on *Donahue* or one of the hundreds of other television appearances she made that year. Perhaps they had written to Shere as well.

This letter is typical of the thousands that Shere received from women after *The Hite Report* was published in September 1976. It was precisely this kind of woman Shere wanted to reach. As the book climbed the bestseller list, she told the reporters who interviewed her for newspapers and TV that as a 'daughter of Middle America', she wanted the book to get to women like her mother and her grandmother whose lives, she felt, were ruled by a double standard. She wanted to bring the women's movement to the women of the American suburbs, 'to free them, make them have more fun, be more sensual, more brave'. Her editor, Regina Ryan, was aligned with this vision. She told me, from 'the first minute I heard what [Shere] was doing, [I knew] that it was for a general market. The book was for a general reader . . . It wasn't going to be a little niche feminist book. It was for all women, that was easy, a no-brainer, from a publishing point of view'. The success of *The Hite Report* went far beyond any other book Ryan worked on across her illustrious publishing career. But at the time, 'nobody could have imagined how big it would be', and it almost didn't happen.

For the book to have a wide reach, Shere became a one-woman promotion machine. The publicity Macmillan offered her was inadequate. In her words: 'Just before the book came out . . . it became clear to me that there was very little publicity being planned'. Macmillan had given the book to 'a 22 year old brainless man in the publicity department' who had 'ten other books to publicize that month' and who turned down an offer of an interview on behalf of Shere because he thought the book would be 'too ticklish for television'. She took matters into her own hands. She went to the Macmillan offices after the staff had gone home and stayed until midnight each night, 'addressing envelopes . . . making photocopies, and generally trying to get together some press material'. She worked at night because 'during the daytime I was made to feel in the way'. Right before the book went to print, Macmillan told her they were decreasing the print run to just four and a half thousand copies. 'They told me female sexuality had been over-discussed . . . and nobody needed any new books about it. Sorry kid'. Her boyfriend, Martin Sage, was with her when she got the news. He described the scene vividly: 'She was livid . . . She smashed her thrift shop dishes with her pink "Princess" phone. I had never seen a woman express that level of anger'. She was furious because even if all 4,500 copies of the book sold, that minuscule run was not enough to get her out of debt. She had also spent thousands of hours on the book. She had drawn conclusions that had the power to reshape sexual lives right across the United States, but only if people could find out about them.

She workshopped with Sage, who knew a thing or two about media. Before editing *Sexology*, he worked at the *New York Post*. He was a community organiser and successfully 'helped unite tree-lined West 86th Street in its fight against the opening of a McDonald's' right next to his house. He knew that 'a press conference makes things news. You have to draw a bunch of journalists together, not try to approach them one by one' as Shere had been, sending letters out individually at Macmillan. Instead, 'you have to create enough of a hubbub . . . among a bunch of journalists, then they all have to cover it for fear that they'll be missing something', he said. They organised a press conference for the book's release. Sage pulled in all of his media contacts, colleagues from the *Post*, a friend from the *New York Times*, someone he had once asked out at *Newsweek*. Sage and Shere's relationship was not always harmonious; she was working all the time and could be quite volatile. 'You would say something totally innocuous—like "I'm going to move this glass because it's dripping"—and she would lose her temper', seeing it as a personal attack. But he recalled that during this period, they were 'a couple that was always smiling at one another'.

Shere decided to hold the press conference as a feminist panel discussion, and contacted women she knew from the movement. The press release was titled 'Women for a New Sexuality'.It included four other feminists, including Kay Whitlock, who coordinated the NOW task force on sexuality and lesbianism, and Leah Schaefer, a psychotherapist specialising in women and sex. Shere framed it as a feminist event because, as Sage explained, 'if she could show that she had the support of feminist voices, that would also make her points more meaningful to the [wider] population'. The naysayers at Macmillan said it would be a disaster, but one hundred people came along. Thirty-six journalists showed up, thirty-five women and one man, representing almost all the major newspapers and magazines. The speakers situated *The Hite Report* within a larger feminist project that saw sexuality as key to the liberation of women. Shere's contribution was to 'publicly declare . . . , on the basis of a large sample . . . that most women do not orgasm from simple coitus', for the first time ever. She and the other speakers answered questions from the press. Some of these were hostile: Wasn't the focus on clitoral stimulation a bit militant? Was the book 'holding up masturbation as a glorious affair?' In the archive is a note that Shere likely passed to Schaefer during the press conference with the instruction 'Leah Be a Good Girl!' 'What a day', Shere reflected later. But it was only the beginning.

The book was praised by the *New York Times*. It reported that most women required clitoral stimulation to orgasm. The public hadn't necessarily heard the word 'clitoris' before, so the article explained, 'it is a pea-sized hooded organ above the vagina'. But it was feminist Erica Jong's write-up for the *New York Times Book Review* that put *The Hite Report* on the map. Regina Ryan organised this, and described it as 'my big coup'. Ryan explained that the *Book Review* had initially appointed a feminist scientist to review *The Hite Report*. She was critical of the book because it was 'unscientific'—a charge that would dog Shere across her life. But the reviewer 'didn't want to pan it'. The *Book Review* usually maintained a distance from editors and publishing houses to encourage robust critique and ensure impartiality, 'like a wall'. But the editor at the *Book Review* who knew Ryan called her to say, '"We've got a problem here"'. Then Ryan called Erica Jong. It was 'like a feminist mafia'.

Jong's review focussed on the way the book gave voice to women's feelings, describing it as a 'culmination' of a very revolutionary trend in the women's movement to let 'women speak in their own words about what they liked, disliked, felt, thought'. To her, women's widespread sexual dissatisfaction demonstrated that society was starved of sex rather than satisfied and satiated, despite the sexual revolution. She urged men and women to 'read it to find out how sex is now'. Suddenly, everyone wanted a piece of Shere.

Shere embarked on a relentless nine-month tour across the United States. She took a democratic approach. She would go on any television show, speak to any newspaper, on any radio station, from *Good Night America* and *The Phil Donahue Show* to local radio, from *Homemaker's Magazine* to *Vogue* to *Playboy*. In the archive, there are huge lists of media outlets she intended to contact, magazines she hoped to appear in. Often these lists are written on hotel stationery, on the backs of airline tickets, customs forms, and luggage tags. One bears the directive in capitals, 'SEND PACKET TO ALL MAJOR TALK SHOWS'. I imagine she flew from city to city, did several interviews, got to her hotel, sat at the desk, looked out at some skyline or, more likely, a brick wall, and worked late into the night, making lists of people to contact, planning her next media appearances.

After four years 'working all day and night, seven days a week feverishly', of course she wanted the book to be successful and widely known. She had to be ambitious. But she went above and beyond. Along with the press work, she sent *The Hite Report* out to important women of America. She sent a copy and a handwritten note to Mary Costa, the voice of Princess Aurora in the 1959 Disney film *Sleeping Beauty*, who replied just as you might expect with a thank-you on stationery fit for a princess—gold, white, and gauzy. She sent a copy to the White House via Midge Costanza, then assistant to President Jimmy Carter, who liaised with the women's movement. Costanza assured Shere she was looking forward to reading it. Shere never stopped, because her whole identity was riding on the book being lauded. She had always wanted to be taken seriously as a researcher. After her plans for grad school were scuppered, she went it alone, which made it more difficult to get the respect she wanted and deserved. More than respect, though, she wanted acceptance. As Martin Sage put it, 'She didn't feel loved as a child. If she could get the love of a population, it would go some way to making her feel whole'. Seeking adoration, she bound her sense of worth to the notoriously fickle American media. 'She was really an aspiring rock star', Sage said. 'She really wanted that adulation. And she wanted it to be unlimited'.

In her early interviews, she is pretty green. Dylan Landis, who helped with the book, watched Shere's first television appearance after it had been published. Shere had called Landis, hoping she might sit in the studio audience and ask a 'friendly question'. Landis had declined: 'I might have been the kind of person who would walk up to a person at a conference and say, "I want to work for you for free"', as she did with Shere, but 'I was not the kind of person who was going to stand up in front of TV cameras' for any reason, least of all if she 'had to ask a question which included the word "clitoris"'. She told Shere she couldn't do it. Shere was disappointed, and Landis felt bad letting her down. But she tuned in to Shere's appearance from her dorm at Barnard. The first thing she saw, she told me, was 'her picking at a thread at the hem of her skirt. I was telegraphing to her, "Sherry, take your hand away from the hem of your skirt. Just take your hand away and let it lie still in your lap . . ." My heart went out to her. It did not look professional. I knew she urgently needed to project authority to those who were going to challenge her and her work'.

Interviewers were not sure what to make of this woman who was a former nude model, a graduate school dropout who '[dressed] like Tinkerbell' with her mass of frizzled blond hair and shiny red lips, but who was now a 'right-on radical'. She dressed this way because she loved vintage clothes and beautiful things and because she absolutely did not want to look like anyone else. But to the media, she seemed like a woman who had mastered the art of being an object. She had learnt 'to survey everything she is, and everything she does because how she appears to others, and ultimately how she appears to men' is crucial to 'the success of her life', as John Berger wrote of life lived in the glare of the male gaze.[1] Shere appeared as a shiny bauble, until she spoke about her work and her research findings. Then she demanded that all women deserved sexual pleasure; they were subjects, not objects. She was unafraid to say 'female orgasm', unembarrassed to say 'clitoris'. She stabbed the male gaze in the eye with her pink pearl hairpin.

Despite the extravagant costuming, Shere's affect was often flat, her face quite inexpressive. She spoke about the clitoris and the orgasm in low and modulated tones. Her interviews have lately been remixed into 'unintentional ASMR' videos. In clips, she doesn't really relate or nod along to the questions. Sometimes she looks bored, slouched in her chair, or distracted, like there were a hundred other places she had to be. Martin Sage suggested she was nervous it wouldn't go well, and so 'stepped outside of herself'; she wasn't bored, but disassociated. If offered a compliment about her book, Shere's face usually remained rigid and inexpressive as a statue. Anything nice anyone said seemed to fall off her, the way her long-drop clip-on earrings threatened to. But if she cracked an unexpected smile or laughed 'like a windchime', her whole face lit up and she came back into view.

SHERE'S MEDIA BLITZ DID THE trick. *The National Observer* described *The Hite Report* as 'a bombshell'—apt, as it exploded sex forever. *Cosmopolitan* declared it 'more myth-shattering than anything since Masters and Johnson, more liberating that the ERA [Equal Rights Amendment]!' Even *Playboy* gave the book a fair shake. They fretted that the book's focus on masturbation would 'make men obsolete', but they wrote of Shere, who had once posed naked for them, that 'her most revolutionary contribution' was the way she redefined *orgasm*. 'Thanks to *The Hite Report:* the man does not give the woman her orgasm: it is something she works toward herself'. In the first year, the book sold two and a half million copies. By 1977, ninety-nine thousand copies were selling every month, and by March it had spent twenty weeks on the *New York Times* bestseller list. Karen Durbin from *Mademoiselle* phoned Macmillan to get a review copy, but 'the warehouse was already empty, so were the local bookstores . . . they had ordered heavily then sold out within two days. At $12.50 a pop . . . that's fairly remarkable'.

To celebrate, Shere held a party at the UN Plaza Hotel in New York. All those who worked with her and supported the book came. Shere passed out cheques to clear her debts, to Virginio the doorman, and to old boyfriends whom she had borrowed money from. Shere ordered a huge three-tiered cake, wedding white and decorated with spun sugar rosebuds. In the pictures, the tiers are sinking into one another and threatening to slide off the table. Her outfit matched the cake, of course. She wore a white Victorian blouse by Zandra Rhodes, layered with a dress made from a damask curtain. She told the journalist covering the event for the *New York Times* that you could tell it was a curtain because 'the roses are upside down in [the] back'. The cake was iced with the first names of those who lent Shere money, like Martin, and those who helped with the research, like Dylan, who sat next to Shere in a thrift-store wrap blouse. In the photo, Shere smiles widely, surrounded by people who love her, who are smiling too, drinking and helping themselves to the pâté. She cuts the cake messily, and I hope she licked the buttercream off the tips of her manicured nails. She looks very genuinely happy, one of the rare times that she does. She's pictured with other people, which is also rare. Of course it's a celebration of her, her book, her vision, and her tireless efforts to finish her book, but it's also a celebration of a collective project, and of feminism as a political movement. In her planning notes, she'd hoped it would be a party 'in celebration and sisterhood fr.[om] 3000 w.[omen] to the women of the world'. In the centre of the cake, '3000 women' was written in icing, celebrating those anonymous women who filled out surveys, the party in their honour as well.

Letters started flooding in to Shere from readers all over the country. Women wrote to Shere to tell her how difficult it was to get a copy of the book. Women drove from bookstore to bookstore, or were on the list at the library for months before they finally got their hands on *The Hite Report*. One woman wrote to tell her she had driven to the San Francisco airport, bought the entire stock, filled the trunk of her car with copies, and distributed the book to her friends across state lines. Shere got letters from all kinds of readers, from a cook on a Mississippi riverboat, from scientists and sex workers, from Quakers, secretaries, and factory workers. One wrote: 'I am writing this on my coffee break at work which has now been over for ten minutes'.

The largest group of correspondents was women in the suburbs. Shere had reached the women she hoped to reach. While doing the shopping, one woman saw the book at the grocery store among the potboilers aimed at men: 'I thought "oh shit, just what we need, another sex survey to tell us how abnormal we all are" but then I noticed the author's name (a woman?!) and on the strength of that I handed over $2.75 of my hard earned cash . . . I believe it was now one of my more worthwhile investments'. One writer penned a note on stationery headed with her husband's name: 'I have spent the last twelve years feeling less than normal, dreading each new sexual contact and the explanations I would eventually have to make for being unable to orgasm normally. When I recall all the ridiculous apologies I've made and the doctors I've seen, I could scream. You have changed my life forever'. These feelings of normalcy were accompanied by relief: 'This book gives a marvellous feeling, of "thank goodness, I'm not the only woman who feels like this . . . " It's a great sigh and wipe of the brow'. Another woman wrote: 'I identified, laughed, I cried, but most important I'm convinced I'm not abnormal. It's the greatest relief in my life'.

WHAT DO SHERE'S CORRESPONDENTS MEAN when they write, over and over, 'I feel normal'? The 'normal' is a powerful idea. It can seem like it has always been with us, like perhaps there has always been a broad, overarching scheme of normality to compare ourselves to and wonder how we measure up, particularly when it comes to sex. But in actuality, it is a relatively new way of explaining the world, a fairly novel anxiety. So, while women wrote to Shere stating that she had helped them to feel sexually normal, a hundred years earlier this would not have been the way they understood themselves, their lives, and the sex they were having. There would have been no scale of comparison, no norm or average that people were constantly measuring themselves against. Instead, they would have used divisions like *natural versus unnatural* or *proper versus improper.*

The idea of 'normal' was born from the boom in statistics collected by governments, from medicine and eugenics and the racist colonial expansion of the nineteenth century. Historians suggest it was through eugenics that the mathematical notion of the normal meaning 'average' and the medical concept of the normal meaning 'healthy' converged and became culturally dominant. This replaced, at least in part, the old system of rigid binaries where you were either one or the other, with a scale, or spectrum, where people could be more or less normal, closer to the middle or dwelling at the edges. As historians Peter Crye and Elizabeth Stephens convincingly show, it was in the twentieth century that the power of the normal really began to be felt. It was through literature on sex and psychology that the 'normal' swirled through the culture and became 'a precarious and elusive state that must be actively cultivated', a desire held by everyday people, particularly when it came to their sex lives.[2]

When women wrote to Shere celebrating that they were normal, I think they meant that they were one of the majority, that is, statistically likely. They saw themselves in the statistic Shere gives of the 70 percent of women unable to orgasm from vaginal penetration, and they saw themselves reflected in other's women's testimonies too, on every page of the *Report*, as some said in their letters. But this bled into a second meaning; 'normal' meant they were fine, and they felt relieved and happy about that. 'Normal', then, was something good for these women; it meant socially acceptable and valued. To read these letters is to see the idea of sexual normalcy changing before our eyes. The idea of the 'normal' orgasm was changing from vaginal to clitoral, and with it the kinds of sex women could have, even the people they might be. Seeing this norm change shows us that 'normal' is not fixed, impartial, or common sense. Instead, it is political, often reflective of what the ruling minority finds desirable. As one woman wrote, 'Up until now we have had to rely mainly on men to define what is "normal"'. As we saw in the previous chapter, psychologists, sexologists, and doctors, along with husbands and male partners, had told women they were abnormal because of their lack of vaginal orgasm, their desire to masturbate or have sex with women.

Today, many of us are sceptical of the very idea of the 'normal'. It seems oppressive and something to avoid, especially as the far right mobilise around the concept. Eric Kaufman, a right-wing intellectual, writes that 'If politics in the West is ever to return to normal, rather than becoming even more polarized, white interests will need to be discussed'.[3] Similarly, participants in the violent protests in Britain and Northern Ireland against asylum seekers in the summer of 2025 suggest that the protests are 'what happens when you get normal people like us and no-one listens to them'.[4] 'Normal' is doing heavy lifting here; it is used to legitimise the racism of the right as the values of the majority, so we distance ourselves from it.

Normal sex, too, seems drearily conformist, but this is a result in shifts from the left rather than the right of politics. Queer theory and culture has waged war on normal, not just on particularly restrictive and oppressive norms but the entire concept of normal sexual behaviour.[5] While Shere's book replaced one idea of normal sex with another that was more liberating to many women, queer theory challenged the idea of the 'normal' entirely and showed that while the 'normal' was a spectrum, it still relied on certain people being pathologized and excluded as 'abnormal'. But contra our feelings today, these letters show us how a sense of 'being normal' can inspire political change.

These feelings of normalcy inspired women to speak up in sex, to try masturbating, and to change their lives. Many women spoke of how the book helped them be more direct in sex: 'I am basically inarticulate with my husband, your book helped change that'. Sometimes speaking up led to things changing, quite rapidly: 'your book has caused what I can only refer to as a major miracle in my life. The day after I finished it I had the extreme pleasure of experiencing the first orgasm I have ever had during intercourse after more than 20 years of nothing and worse than nothing'. When they found out that other women masturbated, they cast off their own feelings of guilt or tried masturbation for the first time, often using the book as erotic material: 'After reading, I decided I must have been crazy to go my whole life without trying to masturbate. So I tried and WHAM, I came within four minutes'. Another woman wrote, 'Tonight I found my clitoris! Such a beautiful pearl I've never seen before'. The book also made her feel that her lesbian desires were normal, and she ended with a P.S.: 'I'm 86'.

This feeling of belonging inspired women to make changes beyond their sex lives. Reassured that they were normal, women felt part of a community with one another: 'I feel so close to womankind, a wonderfully warming feeling'; 'I laughed and laughed about some of the quotes because they were exactly my experience. I wanted to dash out and find the women quoted so we could laugh together'. As we saw in chapter two, Shere wanted the book to be like a consciousness-raising group. I think she had women in the suburbs in mind here, women who may not have had access to CR in person but would get the feeling of the group through reading stories of women's similar lives. Like CR, the book challenged women's politics; one reader, a 'closet woman hater', now felt a genuine sense of closeness to other women, because of 'this marvellous book—glory be'. Another woman who had always thought of lesbian relationships as 'disgusting' was beginning to consider the possibility for herself. 'This is what your book is doing—giving people a chance to think over relationships [beyond] what is culturally ingrained in their heads'. While reading was an individual experience, women built community where they were. One woman told Shere she was 'like your no.2 PR person' because she told so many friends about it. Another wrote that she was 'passing the book around my office for everyone to read'. She reported that lots of the 'ladies are reading it with the book hidden so that no one else knows they are reading "that kind of book." But I am not ashamed'.

The Hite Report was a bold feminist book, but it appealed to these women because it required no prior knowledge of feminism. It was practical, with suggestions about how women could change their sex lives for the better by applying feminist principles, without needing to adopt an entire feminist programme, though because of the book some of them did. One woman who wrote several letters to Shere over a ten-year period joined her local NOW chapter after reading *The Hite Report*. She became an active organiser for reproductive rights. In the last letter she sent to Shere, she attached two small badges in the shape of coat hangers, symbolising women's refusal to return to a time of unsafe illegal abortions. 'Never again', she wrote.

The book's reception changes the story we tell about feminism. Usually, the history of this extraordinary social movement is located in the cities and on university campuses. The suburbs are seen as the place where women were trapped in their houses and isolated, where ideas of what a 'normal' woman was pressed heavily upon their lives. Maintaining normal standards could have a violent edge, as in the horror novel *The Stepford Wives*, where women are killed off by their own husbands, replaced by automatons who glide around the supermarket declaring 'housework is enough for me' and who always orgasm vaginally. Suburban women would soon be mobilised by the New Right, which claimed normal women had been silenced by feminism. But *The Hite Report* changes the story; it shows how feminism did reach right into the heart of the suburbs, changing sexual norms and the lives of these allegedly 'normal' women.

TO BE SURE, NOT EVERYONE fit Shere's new version of the 'normal' woman, not because of the way they had orgasms but because Shere's idea of a 'normal' woman was a white woman. Shere, like many white feminists of the 1970s, understood gender as the primary oppression in women's lives, from which all other oppressions such as class and race were born. At the time *The Hite Report* was published, Black feminists suggested that when the women's movement referred to 'women' it actually meant white women, but this whiteness was rarely mentioned. White women came to stand in for all women, their very specific experience universalised, their whiteness invisibilised in the idea of 'woman'.[6]

This is true in *The Hite Report*. The questionnaire was an iterative process. In the first version, Shere did not ask about women's age, religious background, education, occupation, or race at all because 'so many survey results have given the impression of categorizing and labelling people on a superficial basis'. It was hoped that by not asking these types of questions she could 'break through to a deeper level of communication with the person answering', something that many women did appreciate. In the second version, she asked, 'What is your age and background—occupation, education, upbringing, race, or anything you may consider important?' She published data in *The Hite Report* on education and occupation, but race goes unanalysed in her study.

BLACK WOMEN'S EXPERIENCES OF SEX were often invisible to white feminists like Shere. Roberta Sykes, a Black Australian feminist, found the way white feminists 'chatter[ed] on about sexual oppression and the competitive orgasm' particularly irrelevant to Black women.[7] Some Black feminists saw the focus on sexual pleasure as a bourgeois concern, part of a repertoire of idle dreams indulged in by the white housewife, who may have been trapped in the suburbs but at least had a mind that could wander. Dreams of sexual liberation were not the priority of Black women who had to work, often for poverty wages, their minds occupied with the worries of the racialised poor.[8] More deeply, Black women were wary about investing in ideas of sexual pleasure as *The Hite Report* encouraged, considering that the history of sexual exploitation of Black women was a key part of enslavement and colonisation. As we have seen, this led to the racist stereotype of Black women being viewed as lascivious, oversexed, and unrapable. This had huge impact on the lives of Black women then, and now.

What do we do with *The Hite Report* after we begin to see how Shere's 'normal' woman is a white woman? Is there a way to acknowledge the book's insights, which took feminism into the heart of America, whilst also acknowledging the book's blind spots and racism, in a way where neither supersedes the other? It seems important that we do hold *The Hite Report* this way. If we discard the book, we risk not understanding why women were so attached to it, why this book was so important to them, why it sold fifty million copies and was translated around the world. If we discard the book, we also miss something else—something surprising and interesting—and that is the contribution of Black women to *The Hite Report* and their letters to Shere.

WOMEN OF COLOUR DID CONTRIBUTE to *The Hite Report*. Shere wrote that 'a small number of women identified themselves by race' in their questionnaires, so I went to look for these in the archive. Most women who filled out the survey didn't offer extensive reflections on how their sex lives were determined by race; that is true of women of colour as well as white women. I don't think this means that race wasn't woven into this most intimate realm, though. Black feminist thought makes it clear that it definitely was, but it wasn't prioritised in the questionnaire, so couldn't be prioritised by those who filled it out. One Black woman recorded her response on tape, which she sent to Shere. To hear her talk about sex and relationships, her children and her studies, is a very intimate listening experience. Her voice sometimes thickens with emotion or drops to a whisper to avoid being overheard. In the background, noises of everyday life—the vacuum cleaner, the television, laughter—are present. On the recording, she reflected on why Black women didn't always discuss sexual oppression with white feminists: 'I think [Black women] have always been torn, we don't want to put our men down . . . Most Black women are removed from the white women's movement, though we agree with some of the goals. It's a very tricky situation to not want to hurt the Black male, yet not wanting that male patriarchy to dominate us'.

Women of colour thought through how the entanglements of race and gender determined their so-called normal sexual experiences and how racism too snuck between the sheets with both men of colour and white men. On her tape, the woman remarked: 'My beauty has never been recognised. When I was growing up, Black women had no beauty'. A young Black law student wrote that she 'couldn't screw across barriers', that white men didn't desire her. This reflected a sexual politics based on a racialised hierarchy where white women are placed above women of colour because 'white men have less to gain in terms of social status by fucking Black women', as philosopher Amia Srinivasan put it.[9] One woman noted that her ethnicity as a Chinese American made a difference to her sex life: 'Everything does'. She commented that as global politics had changed, so had her partners' sexual preferences. More men had a fetish for Asian women because 'Chinese is "in" this year', she noted sardonically. Philosopher Robin Zheng shows that racial fetishes are not just a matter of pure aesthetic preferences but based on racial stereotypes. Men come with expectations of how Asian women should look and act, which Asian women then have to negotiate in their relationships.[10] Shere argued that for sex to be really good, feminism was required; the women of colour who filled out her survey push her project further by saying racism too would have to end if sex is to be its most erotic.

These women show that racist sexual stereotypes aren't entirely determining. The Chinese American woman quoted above also reflected on her love of sex and masturbation. Of all the respondents, she is particularly clear-eyed and unashamed. She is a woman who really knows what she is about: 'I decided long ago that I would not, could not waste time waiting to be asked, so I do initiate. In the process, I also eliminate people who are turned off by "aggressive" women'. She described 'well-written, literate porn' as the 'greatest', and was enjoying the Victorian pornographic magazine *The Pearl*. This was 'a little on the sexist side . . . matter of fact, a lot on the sexist side, but very exciting'. She was also particularly thoughtful about the way that power played out in sex. In response to the question 'what do you think of sado-masochism?' she replied 'whips and leather and bondage turn my stomach rather than turn me on [but] there is usually a certain amount of domination/submission in all sexual encounters. Sometimes I like to get off on dominating, and sometimes I like to be dominated . . . in a good relationship, one can play all the roles'. Lesbian and bisexual women of colour discussed their positive feelings about sex. One Black bisexual feminist spoke in glowing terms about having a woman lover. She reflected, 'I like tall, thin people with long legs. My men must have a quiet softness about them, a gentle loving quality, a dreamy far-awayness like Don Quixote. My women should be brash, open vivacious and very with it, like Germaine Greer'. As Alice Walker's poem is titled, '"Women of Color" Have Rarely Had the Opportunity to Write About Their Love Affairs', but these women took the opportunity by writing to Shere.[11] Their letters and surveys reveal these women's lives, loves, and feelings, and feelings about sex in all their full, complex humanity.

The Hite Report's blind spots don't just come into view retrospectively; some women noticed them at the time. One reader pointed out that Shere's idea of a 'normal' woman was nondisabled. 'I loved your book . . . I insist that all of my boyfriends read it. After they do, they suddenly become more understanding, more romantic and fun to be with'. But, 'your survey of women was basically only answered by "physically normal (?)" women. How about those that aren't? . . . I admit to having a personal stake in this game. I am what some might consider severely handicapped, though most people I meet don't seem to notice it', and, she added, it doesn't 'interfere with my sexual activities'. She reflected on how she and other disabled people were dehumanised because 'the idea of having a handicapped individual as a sex partner is never even considered by the majority of the public . . . the handicapped are considered beings who do not experience the same emotions as other[s]'. People don't expect that 'they have a fully intact libido. Well of course they do!' To further challenge sexual norms, this woman wanted to develop, distribute, and analyse a survey about disabled people's sex lives. She felt well placed to do so because she was part of a community of disabled people and because, she said, 'I have a lot of guts and can take a certain amount of bad mouthing'. She asked Shere for advice: 'How in the world am I going to be able to correlate all of the answers so they mean something? I hope you can just at least give me a clue on how to start so maybe I can figure it out along the way'. She hoped that her survey would make people 'realize that most handicapped persons are not handicapped when it comes to being responsive and generally fun sex partners'. To her credit, Shere tried over and over to get in touch with this woman via phone and mail—her scribbled notes in a range of colours say as much—but as far as I know, they never made contact. Shere certainly did replace the sexist norm of vaginal intercourse with another, which was more liberating, but within it lay the idea of a 'normal' woman who was white and able-bodied. *The Hite Report* did, however, lay important groundwork for others to extend normal sex in terms of what was done and who was doing it, including eventually the challenge mounted by queer theory and culture in the 1990s that tried to do away with the normal altogether.

While women felt liberated by the newfound sense of normalcy gained from reading *The Hite Report*, critics in the media accused Shere and the women she surveyed of being abnormal. Some reporters suggested that the sample was biased, the study not accurate or scientific. They charged that a woman who took the time to answer a fifty-seven-item questionnaire on the topic of sexual pleasure 'has to be unusual and/or weird'. On talk shows, interviewers wondered aloud if 'what emerges from the book . . . is 3,000 desperately to moderately unhappy women, women who are not getting what they want . . . Aren't they the ones who are likely to reply to this questionnaire?' What this amounted to was saying in fact that actually, *normal* women *do* orgasm vaginally after all, and so nothing need change between men and women sexually. Shere reminded the media that the book had been read widely and that the thousands of letters she received from women corroborated her findings. If there were lots of women who were having vaginal orgasms, surely she would have heard from them?

More than this, Shere said, 'there had never been a perfect sample in sex research'. Kinsey undertook studies on mostly white, middle-class people. Freud extrapolated his findings about women from a small group of female patients. Random samples are most accurate, but in sex research, this type of survey has not been possible because most of the people chosen at random would not answer due to the subject matter. She wrote that in random samples the questions are often multiple choice, 'the answers pre-standardized, or if you want to be more cynical, pre-biased'. Sometimes multiple-choice questions '*tell* [. . .] people what to think—rather than *ask* them'.

Shere did find it difficult to take criticism. Even in interviews that were overwhelmingly positive, that allowed her time to get the ideas out and complimented her on the work, there was likely to be some critique. Watching the recordings, I see that she looks devastated in these moments, her heart right on the sleeve of her angora sweater or high-necked Victorian blouse. As Dylan Landis put it, 'sometimes she looked like she was made of glass'. Her face falls, she bites the end off the question, sees it as a fatal misunderstanding or a personal attack. Sometimes, if she felt the interviewer was dwelling too long on one thing, she walked off in a huff or put the phone down.There was so much riding on the success of the book that she could be very defensive.

The worst review was from *Hustler*, the porn mag that prided itself on being more hardcore than *Playboy*. This was the first really personal attack on Shere, a harbinger of things to come. *Hustler*'s April 1977 cover screamed, 'Shere Hite Nude! The Hite Report Exposed'. They reproduced six half-page photographs that were sold to them by Sam Menning, who photographed Shere in 1968, aiming to sell the pictures to the sex shops that lined 42nd Street. The shoot took place in a hotel room that you might pull into off the motorway, cheap and hot with dusty lace curtains, former guests' hair on the pillows. You can see the coffee maker and the telephone in the background. Shere lies on a bright blue-and-green acrylic bedspread in various poses, legs spread, on all fours, growling like a lion. She looks like someone who has been asked to 'do a sexy look', and she looks pretty tired. She wears a green feather boa on her head, sometimes a wig, sometimes pink crotchless underwear, mostly nothing. It does not look fun, it does not look glamorous.

The accompanying article was brutal. As *Hustler* saw it, Shere couldn't possibly understand normal women or normal sex, because she was a feminist: 'Would you have your plumbing installed by a chef? . . . *The Hite Report* is a major disappointment, filled with faulty data, contradictions and feminist bullshit . . . Hite couldn't resist pleasing the dykes at NOW'. The article insinuated that Shere's work in porn undermined her researcher credentials: 'The new sex guru . . . doesn't want to talk about her past "because when you say 'model' people think you are frivolous." We can see from these photos why people might think that of her . . . But frivolous is too kind a word to describe how Hite has treated her work'. They mock her for her poverty too: 'Apparently attention to detail has never been one of Hite's strong points as is evidenced in her tacky appearance for these photos . . . But you have to admit her filthy feet give her that "lived-in" look, and the cheap wig she's wearing looks like it was lived in by a pack of vermin'. To her conclusion that women are scared to ask men what they want because of inequality, they make a sexual threat dressed up as a joke, as they so often are: 'Come on Shere, all you need to do is ask, and the entire male staff of *Hustler* will gratify you—simultaneously'.

The reproduction of these photos by *Hustler*—which Shere received no extra money for—resembles revenge pornography, wherein a person, usually a woman, consents to their partner taking nude or pornographic photos of them and then, after the relationship breaks down, these images are circulated without her consent on the internet by an aggrieved ex to people known to her, like friends, family, and colleagues. Initially,

Shere did consent to the images being taken by Menning. There are sad little cheques in the archives for $25 and $35 that she received for the shoots, about $200 and $300 today. At that time, she wasn't Shere Hite author of *The Hite Report*, but just a woman who needed to make rent and found porn more lucrative than modelling.

While we might think of revenge porn as a decidedly twenty-first-century phenomenon, these images of Shere were humiliating and dehumanising in the same way. Their republication reduced her from being an author of a bestselling book, a person with preferences and complexities, to an object whose personhood did not matter, someone who is ultimately, only, and no matter what she does, a sexual object to be used for others' purposes. In the memorable words of philosopher Martha Nussbaum, she is reduced to 'something that it is permissible to break up, break apart, smash . . .'[12] In December 1977, Larry Flynt, the owner of *Hustler*, sent Shere a telegram: 'I hope you find it in your heart to forgive me'. I'm not sure how Shere was supposed to accomplish that gargantuan emotional feat, particularly given that *Hustler* once again reproduced the images in 1981, in time for the publication of *The Hite Report on Male Sexuality*, under the headline 'Hite of Absurdity'. As the book was published around the world, these images were printed again and again, like a recurring bad dream. This pulled Shere down to earth, and in a way made her an entirely 'normal' woman, subject to the same kind of sexual subjugation that so many of us are, despite her fame and success.

I HOPE AT THAT TIME Shere was able to say a loud 'Fuck *Hustler*', because *The Hite Report* did catapult Shere into an extraordinary life, well beyond the lives of the 'normal' women who read her book. While Shere's contract with Macmillan had an income limitation clause, capping her earnings at $25,000 a year, this was still upwards of $140,000

Shere as a child in St. Joseph, Missouri, mid-1940s
Schlesinger Library, Harvard Radcliffe Institute

Portrait of Shere, 1970
Mike Wilson

Shere in the kitchen of her basement flat, 1970s
Arthur Schatz

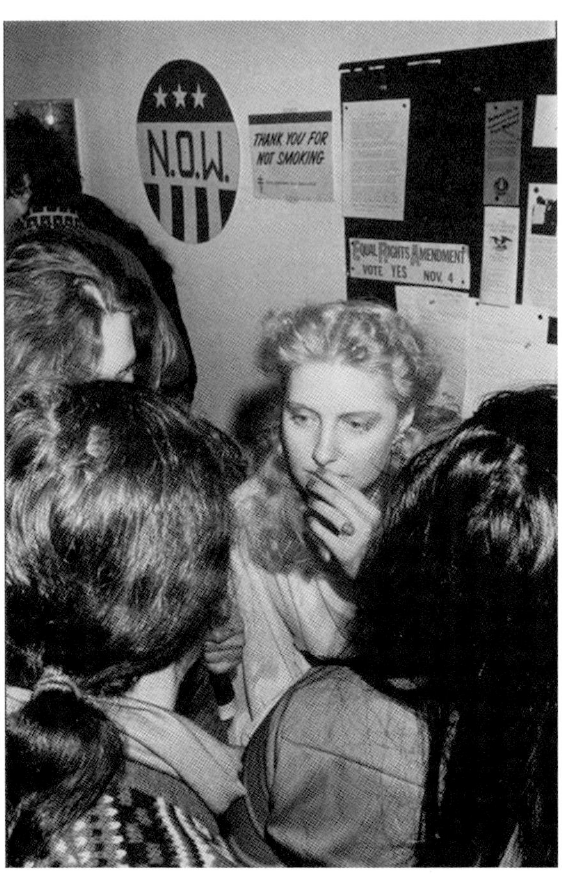

Shere at NOW meeting, 1970s
Bettye Lane

Shere at work, 1976
Bettye Lane

Promotional material for *The Hite Report* designed by Shere, 1977
Schlesinger Library, Harvard Radcliffe Institute

Shere feeling the media pressure, 1995
John Stoddart/Popperfoto

Shere Hite, rock star, 1981
Trevor Leighton/National Portrait Gallery, London

today, more money than she had ever dreamt of. This increased considerably after the book was published by Dell in paperback and after she took Macmillan to court and won, getting a payout of hundreds of thousands of dollars. She began to earn money from the book, which was 'quite a shock' but 'fun'. She moved out of the basement flat into a beautiful residence on Fifth Avenue. 'I bought an apartment!' she wrote in her notes, almost disbelieving. This was no normal apartment. This was just about the furthest you could get from the cold, thin-walled rooms of the house in St. Joseph, or the hotel room from the porn shoot. Far away too from the suburban homes where so many women all across the United States read *The Hite Report*, though these women readers did fund Shere's magnificent new abode. Set over two floors, the ground level was for work. Shere 'hate[d] feeling cramped with papers falling all around [her] head', so this office was light and spacious. It was functionally elegant, with mid-century modernist furniture, light wood floors, white walls, and bookshelves. Shere liked 'significantly big desks, so I got five doors, painted them in pastel colors and put them on filing cabinets all over the room'.

To venture upstairs, though, was to enter what Shere described as 'the bedroom as ballroom'. Regina Ryan described it evocatively when we spoke: 'It was gorgeous, huge windows overlooking Fifth Avenue, it was splendid, it was a splendid apartment. She had an eye, and it was beautifully decorated. She lived beautifully, for a while. She lived rich, for a while'. There are pictures in the archive that Shere used as inspiration for her interior decorating, what we might now call a mood board. This included pictures of the Royal Family at breakfast and photos of 'Aristocratic France' pulled out of the British Airways inflight magazine. In her apartment, there were crystal chandeliers and cherub frescoes, the ornamental plaster was extensive, so was the gilding, the bed was covered with a pink satin quilt. Shere's story is very rags-to-riches, from pauper to princess, *The Hite Report* both her fairy godmother and her handsome prince that she honours with wedding cake; it is this book that woke her—along with so many other women—from their glass coffins, and so in this way, her apartment reminds me of the princess suite in the Walt Disney castle.

Her apartment also recalls Disneyland, or the Palace of Versailles or a stately home, because it's meant to be visited and admired. Her apartment was the backdrop to many parties that Shere hosted. The photos from the time capture the fun and revelry of a masked ball. Ryan remarked that 'She became quite the social person'. She sent party invitations out on her letterhead, *Hite Research* in cursive, the winged deer below. This deer was associated with Shere's favourite goddess, Diana, and represents her power. The stationery is also an exercise in branding: Hite Research was a fictitious research institute—really, it was just Shere—but it gave her a sense of legitimacy, of institutional backing and wealth; the paper is thick, the card is lush, the deer is richly embossed in gold. It was designed by Cartier.

If Shere's apartment was a place to be seen, it was also a place where she could look at herself, her life coming into focus. Suddenly she was doing something that she felt was worthy of her efforts, that she was pleased with, that helped people. Ryan told me that there were 'so many mirrors, mirrors everywhere, it was striking'. Ryan gifted her a mirror for her new apartment that she used as a table. Martin Sage recalled this was quite hard to eat off of because of the raised edges. Ryan suggested that the mirrors 'give you a little hint into her self-interest'. I asked whether she meant that Shere was vain. She laughed, but with real fondness in her voice: 'A little bit. I think she liked to look at herself, she always looked great'. There are notes in the archive about what she hoped to buy along with the apartment: 'Georgia O'Keeffe', 'oil and gas', 'diamonds, paintings, antiques'. 'Can I buy a hotel suite in Paris?' These show us how the American feminist goal of economic independence could congeal into the right to be as rich as any man, to make your own money and spend it exactly how you damn well please. But these notes are flights of fancy. They are not the cold, hard strategizing of those born to wealth; rather, they are the dreams of someone who was haunted by the spectre of poverty and had lived precariously for a long time.

Shere was no longer a 'normal' feminist, going to NOW meetings and hand printing her surveys. She was rich and she was famous, and other feminists began to resent her. British author Hilary Mantel wrote, 'she has offended US feminists by making money out of sisterhood'. Shere felt she was 'accused of being one of those women who profits from the movement, and then rips it off'. This was what New York NOW thought when they sued Shere in 1978. They argued that she had agreed to pay them a substantial amount from sales of *The Hite Report*, in return for using their address and logo on her questionnaires. There was no contract, though she does promise in *The Hite Report* that 'part of any profit which this project may make will be donated to the [NY NOW] chapter'. She hadn't given them money in any meaningful way by the time they sued, just a note with a $50 bill attached for their help collecting the thousands of letters and questionnaires she had distributed. While she thanked them profusely, it's true that she didn't try very hard to keep her promise. NOW argued that the success of the book was down to them, that lending their name 'provided Hite with a valuable asset which enabled her to establish credibility.' Without them she had 'no reputation among women or women's groups as a serious investigator or writer about issues of concern to women', and no one would have filled out the questionnaire. To NOW she had been 'unjustly enriched', and they sued her for $625,000, over $3 million in today's money. Eventually, they settled out of court. Shere gave them $30,000—according to her, a gift she always intended to give. They released a joint press statement. Shere stated 'there were no ill feelings', though she later wrote to the entire organisation that 'the last thing I will ever do, even though I am a feminist from now until forever, is contribute one penny to the National Organization for Women'. In her private writings she noted that 'this has been a v. diff[icult] yr. for me and you have dealt me the final blow. It has made me feel literally suicidal. All of this has hurt me very much. What more can I say except why on earth have you behaved this way?'

Shere wondered if NOW was 'acting out of narrow-minded jealousy' because she was famous. There may be some truth to that. Jealousy was certainly present, though a taboo feeling in a movement that aimed for complete equality among women. While women valued the real talk and honesty of consciousness raising, jealousy within the movement often went undiscussed. It was too shameful, so women denied it in themselves or framed it as political disagreement rather than admitting that this hot, poisonous emotion frothed through them greenly. Gay liberation activist and feminist Martha Shelley comes closest to naming jealousy toward the movement's media stars, who she watched 'ascen[d] into the heavens with an increasing incidence of ulcers and migraine . . . [while] we struggle to get our groups together, working quietly at the day-care centers, on the mimeo machine . . .'[13] When you put it like that, it seems obvious that people who spent their lives in the feminist trenches would be jealous of Shere. Her large parties, conspicuous consumption, ostentatious media appearances, and unimaginable fame would never have happened were it not for a large feminist movement.

But she wasn't just a victim of jealousy. The movement had norms, and Shere was no normal feminist. She courted media attention, published her work with a mainstream publisher, and did not toe the line aesthetically, neither ascribing to the sturdy shoes, dungarees, and work shirt of grassroots feminists nor the fitted suits, pearls, and heels that the respectable women of NOW preferred. The movement also saw her as a sellout, motivated not by women's liberation but 'partly by the desire for fame and fortune, and partly by the desperate need for male attention'. Celebrity feminists like Shere undermined the movement because they made large numbers of women 'passively depend on a few stars to liberate them instead of getting themselves to do it', so 'the movement [would] surely fail'. Yet, when we read the letters from women in the suburbs, we see that Shere inspired not passivity but action toward liberation in women who had never taken these kinds of steps before. Shere challenged the women's movement's ideas of what a feminist was and what she should be, how she should work, look, and behave. But without a mainstream publisher and the mainstream media, who were, it's true, partly interested in her because of her look, the book would never have carried feminism right into the heart of the American suburbs. It would never have changed the kind of sex millions of so-called 'normal' women were having, and changed their lives too.

CHAPTER 4

"WOMEN AROUND THE WORLD LOVE *THE HITE REPORT*!"

In the archive lie several copies of a thick booklet, hand-titled by Shere in her distinctive cursive: 'Women Around the World Love the Hite Report'. This is a collection of newspaper and magazine articles from across the globe applauding *The Hite Report*. Shere put this together in 1977 for media and publishers, after the initial publicity storm waned to a flurry. She wanted to stay in the public eye and keep growing her audience, so she sought to showcase the book's extraordinary worldwide success. The booklet has the feel of a school project. On the title page, Shere affixed small versions of the book's cover in Japanese, Swedish, Italian, Spanish, and the original English, at jaunty angles. She accented them with red and yellow marker and wrote captions below each one, the words crowded together as she ran out of space: 'Now 4 months on bestseller list', '#1 Spain'. In the centre, between the book covers, is Shere, in a feminised Superman costume: She wears a short red skirt, thigh-high boots, and cape, complete with the iconic *S* on her chest that was also, as luck would have it, the first letter of her name. She flies above the world, which tells us exactly who she imagined her reader to be: everyone. Her arm is outstretched in the classic pose of the superhero. Shere the hot, white, sexually liberated, ultra-modern American feminist to the rescue!

It's clear as we follow *The Hite Report* on its global travels that it resonated with women around the world and that many readers went to great lengths to get their hands on a copy, including in places where the book was banned. But the book's global success was also due to the position of the United States as the most influential world power after World War II.[1] Rather than through capturing territory, the preferred mode of earlier empires, the United States exerted its influence through culture; it was 'a market empire, a great imperium with the outlook of a great emporium', as historian Victoria de Grazia puts it.[2] Certainly, the United States also acted as a global strongman pushing back the tide of communism; it interfered in other countries' sovereign politics and broadened its influence by propping up and piloting in dictators, supporting violent coups, and starting wars across the world. But its commodities, laden with American values, helped the United States to launder its image while doing so. Through exporting consumer goods it remade the lives of everyday people and spread its image as the world's most advanced nation, most democratic, most modern, and sometimes even *most feminist*. Shere did not create these global political conditions, but she was entwined within them. They helped the book to travel and influenced her feminism. Often, as Shere-as-Superman suggests, she leant right into these and adopted an imperialist feminism.[3] When it came to the distribution of her book in the Global South, she saw it as a tool of liberation for women there who she understood as being 'behind' those in the United States. She did not consider the possibility that women had developed their own analytic tools, their own lines of political thought based in their own specific contexts. I bring these to light in this chapter so we might make use of them, even if Shere presumed they did not exist at the time. Shere is instructive; sometimes she offers us solutions to some of the intractable problems in contemporary feminism—how to get beyond those who are already convinced of gender justice to reach literally millions of people globally, men and women—and sometimes she is instructive in that she shows us what not to do.

***THE HITE REPORT* IS THE** thirtieth bestselling book of all time. It has sold fifty million copies and been translated into thirteen languages. It outstripped other feminist bestsellers by tens of millions of copies. *Our Bodies, Ourselves*, the feminist health handbook that was translated widely and celebrated for its reach beyond the United States, has sold four million copies.[4] Macmillan made *The Hite Report* a global smash. After the wild success of the book in the States, her publisher saw that they could make money elsewhere and looked to international markets. By 1978, it had been published in ten countries: the United States, the Netherlands, France, West Germany, Spain, Italy, Israel, Japan, Portugal, and Sweden. Australia, Britain, and Brazil would follow the year after. But Shere's contract did not offer her any protection over the content of the book, and there was no clause to ensure a good quality translation. Shere was worried, particularly after she spoke with the *Our Bodies, Ourselves* collective, who told her of the trouble they had with foreign editors. So, 'feeling like an absolute fool', she picked up the telephone at 4.00 a.m., U.S. time and called around to the publishers who would first publish the book in translation. She introduced herself and explained that she 'didn't want the book sensationalized . . . I wanted decent advertising aimed at women, and a sensitive translation by a woman'.

She was particularly concerned about the publicity and marketing. She explained to publishers in Brazil that 'the promotion [should] be constantly directed toward women, as a conversation and a dialogue. Perhaps starting out with a women's day or women's press conference . . . involving many of the outstanding women in your country, [that] would be a way to make the point. Hopefully, medical and feature writers from major media would attend'. Shere reasoned: 'I feel that you will sell twice as many copies [than] if the book is aimed toward men. It is very hard to get women to buy books on sex, and they probably will not buy this one unless they understand that this is for them. But in this way, men will be sure to buy it too' because men would want to know what women were thinking about sex.

Despite her best efforts, publishers often fobbed her off: 'Don't worry about a thing. We'll do a great job', they told her. Publishers didn't always 'keep the spirit of the book intact'. They were interested in it as a moneymaker and often promoted it as a sex book, stripping out the feminism and using trashy and salacious advertising, packaging, and promotion methods. She wrote to her publisher in the Netherlands, when presented with the cover just before it went to press, to say that she was 'displeased that you never consult with me prior to publication regarding the translator . . . or the cover of my book'. 'I think it's sexist to have my name in pink letters. Can't you use something more dignified?' In France, a naked woman adorned the cover of the first edition.

In Italy, the book was bought by Bompiani, a large commercial publishing house that handled the translation and publicity themselves, with no input from Shere. To promote the book, they worked with *L'Espresso*, the most prominent progressive Italian glossy magazine. Bompiani 'sold them the rights to run excerpts of the book before it appeared in bookshops'. They ran a cover to promote *The Hite Report* with two women, naked from the waist up, captioned 'Pleasure'. Inside, the photos were more pornographic, and the article was titled 'Mr Orgasm? There's a Lady Waiting for You'. Local porn mags interested in this sex report republished images of Shere taken years before when she was working in porn. As in the case of *Hustler* reusing these images, she received no money for these. She employed lawyers, who sent cease and desist letters to these magazines asking that the photos be destroyed and returned. In the archive are pornographic images of Shere that have been hole-punched and scrunched up, her face scribbled out. But she worried these magazines were holding on to other images, which would keep being published. In the hope that she might stem the tide of this pornographic promotion, she told publishers that 'if [they] presented the book sensitively [she] would come to their country and help promote it'. She hoped she would sell more copies that way too.

She began her world tour in early spring of 1977, doing the usual Shere Hite media circuit and keeping a relentless schedule, meeting feminists, doing countless interviews, hoping that if women around the world loved *The Hite Report*, so the world might love her too. Her media appearances further ensured a large readership, and there can be no doubt that *The Hite Report* really did resonate with women—and men—who it reached globally. Women across very different contexts reported that they now felt normal, similar to the women in the American suburbs we met earlier. A forty-three-year-old woman living in Milan whose 'time and energy is devoted to taking care of a large family' wrote to Shere, 'I feel a moral obligation to tell you that your *Report* has rehabilitated me in my own eyes. After years of thinking there was something wrong with me, your book has shown I'm normal. Nobody ever gave me a greater gift'. A woman wrote from Utretcht in the Netherlands to tell Shere how she had used the English-language *Hite Report* to bridge the language barrier between her and her lover and show him her lack of vaginal orgasm was typical: 'I tried to tell him he was wrong [about orgasms], but it was very difficult because he's from New Zealand and it's hard to explain these things in English . . . Finally, he accepted the book and went home and read it. When I saw him again . . . We made love until early in the morning that night and even then we could hardly stop. It has been the most sensational experience of my life'.

The book was not available in the communist bloc, though there is some evidence of readers in the archive. A student from East Germany studying filmography at the University of Łódź in Poland told Shere how he had smuggled the book into the East via West Berlin. While this border was officially closed, it remained porous, and visitors from the West smuggled packages by car with clothing, newspapers, and books like *The Hite Report*. This student had saved up for the expensive, 'luxurious' German edition and was not disappointed: 'I'm a man but your report is of great worth to me'. Because Western books were scarce, he passed his copy around to others, including his ex-wife and some 'girls', though he said his 'feministic friends in Westernized Berlin often criticized my using of 'girl' as sexist.

Until recently, sexual life under communist dictatorships was thought to resemble the totalitarian regime in George Orwell's *1984*, where the state has so interfered in private life that 'procreation was an annual formality like the renewal of a ration card' and the orgasm has been abolished.[5] Historians have shown that sexual life in East Germany was in some ways more liberated than the West because the state promoted women's economic independence. This 'did contribute to a unique, noncommodified, perhaps more "natural" and "free", form of sexuality that flourished', as Kristen Ghodsee argues.[6] Yet, as Josie McLellan has found, while intercourse was more equal, it didn't result in broader challenges to the rigid gender roles and compulsory heterosexuality East Germans were subjected to.[7] It was the feminism of *The Hite Report* that these East German readers found refreshing and relieving. This man wrote: 'The girls told me that every girl and especially every man should read it. One said to me, if her boy wouldn't read your report, she would throw him out! (He read it)'. As a good socialist, he hastened to add that he found *The Hite Report* compatible with East German communism. He felt that 'the Marxist theory of revolution is applicable [to] the feminist revolution. I believe the movement for feminism is a great hope'.

Beyond Europe, the book was particularly successful in Japan. It was published by Pacifica Editions, a major publisher and translator of English books. Shere pushed for the book to be translated by feminist Mioko Fujieda, who she knew. She felt Fujieda was well qualified, as she had translated other feminist books, including *The Three Marias* an important text of Portuguese feminism banned by the Salazar dictatorship. But the publisher declined to use Fujieda, claiming Shere 'was in good hands under the translator we have selected', which she wasn't. Initially, Pacifica appointed a male translator—this was the case 'in 8 out of 10 countries' when *The Hite Report* was first translated—who shipped the translation work out to the students he taught at university. Chiz Nakao, a young woman working in foreign rights at Pacifica, phoned Shere to tell her that the current translation 'was so embarrassing and vague that it made no sense'. Nakao agreed to step in and translate. While Nakao did not 'consider herself a feminist', Shere felt that as a young woman who was divorced, and a 'poet in her own right', she certainly understood the problems women faced and the importance of maintaining the book's sexually explicit content and its feminist spirit.

Nakao and Shere talked on the phone often, and wrote letters. Nakao spoke of Shere's 'sincere attachment to the book' in their correspondence, a diplomatic way to put it, given Shere's protectiveness of the book sometimes veered into being controlling. Nakao reassured her that 'I'll try my very best to make it a great book here'. She spent four weeks of her 'own nights and weekends with no pay and no equal recognition retranslating the book'. She did this under the strict control of the official translator, 'who spent literally two days and two nights non-stop supervising the translation'. Nakao and Shere developed a real friendship. As well as discussing the serious business of work, they gossiped about boyfriends in their letters: 'While you were trying to straighten out with Martin, I've been having a hard time with Ted . . .' They discussed health and life too. Nakao was often sick from overwork. Shere sent her lavish gifts, as she often did to those who supported her. She sent a huge bunch of flowers in mauve, lilac, and violet: 'What a nifty surprise!' Nakao wrote. She also sent a purse, which Nakao carried every day. Shere's gifts were often large and ostentatious, like the flowers, something that the eye would be drawn to or, like the purse, something that could be used daily. Both cases brought Shere to mind, and so these were a way of placing herself in the room.

Shere advocated for Nakao at the publishing house. She wrote to Pacifica from the Ritz in Paris, urging the publishers to credit Nakao's for her translation work: 'I am disappointed . . . that Chiz Nakao's name was not included [on the cover]. This is deeply regrettable since we owe her so much time and intelligent work on the book. I know I need not point out how frequently women are not given full credit for the work they do—which makes the situation even more regrettable'. Pacifica responded with a promise they would acknowledge Nakao on future covers; they later said it had been 'forgotten' by the advertising department. Shere pressed them on this over many letters until 'it was admitted that this would overly-embarrass the original male translator'.

Shere toured Japan in June 1977 after *The Hite Report* had come out there. The publisher wrote to her that this 'turned out to be quite a promotion of your book—and the cause!' Shere held a sizable press conference with all the major newspapers and women's magazines. She asked Nakao to contact women in Japan ahead of her visit and show them magazine articles praising her work in the United States. She also sent English-language copies of *The Hite Report* to the press to try to drum up interest. The schedule was hectic; she did up to four interviews a day, across newspapers, magazines, and television, as well as meetings with feminists and parties and dinners with her publisher. If ever there was an hour free, she tried to fill it with yet another media appearance, her itinerary covered in journalists' names and their scribbled contact details. She made a note about presenting herself to the Japanese media: 'look like Grace Kelly'.

The Hite Report was read widely and got to number one in Japan, and of course this was because of Shere's media work, but the book was particularly popular there because of the role of the United States. The States occupied Japan from the end of World War II until 1952. Ostensibly this occupation took place because Japan had formed an alliance with Germany in the war, and so required democratic reform and stabilisation. This was also strategic: 'Japan was the linchpin in an iron noose of American containment in Asia' against communism.[8] It was key in the U.S. line of defence across the Pacific from the Philippines to Japan, and an important base for U.S. wars in Korea and Vietnam. During the occupation, westernisation of culture took place and the market was flooded with consumer goods. A suite of democratic reforms were granted to women, including suffrage, by the American regime. While Japanese women had been agitating for the vote in Japan before the outbreak of World War II, publicising their improved status was key to the propaganda of the operation to instil in all parties a sense that Americans were the liberators of Japanese women. Early in the U.S. occupation of Japan, the *New York Times* ran a piece called 'Out of Feudalism: Japan's Women'. This opened, 'The dawn has slowly begun to break in the Land of the Rising Sun for Japan's most depressed class, the patient plodding Japanese woman'.[9]

At the time of the occupation, U.S. feminists, too, believed that they were there to liberate their Japanese sisters. They saw themselves as 'members of an advanced, civilized, white nation while Japanese women were supposedly trapped in a backward, benighted, Oriental society'.[10] The opinion that U.S. women were modern and further ahead was shared by some Japanese women and lingered into the 1970s. This combined with the desire for U.S. consumer goods made *The Hite Report* very popular in Japan. The letters Japanese readers wrote to Shere reflected this: '*The Hite Report* translated into Japanese has the reputation of future sex among young people', one read. Another woman remarked that she was 'a bit afraid whether your point of view would reach Japanese people . . . It is my sad understanding that general sexual consciousness is surprisingly low . . . in Japan. Rest assured that your . . . book has contributed a great extent to raise Japanese women's blatant consciousness'.

However, the book's reception among feminists in Japan was not completely determined by these Cold War politics. To Shere's credit, whenever she travelled she asked around for feminist contacts so that she might connect to local women's movements. Mioko Fujieda, her translator friend, sent a long list. This included women's groups that sought change through official channels, anti-imperialist feminists who worked to develop a Pan-Asian solidarity movement against U.S. aggression in both Vietnam and Japan, and the Japanese radical feminist movement, ūman ribu (*women's liberation*). While in Japan, Shere met with feminists while giving a talk at Café Honyarado, a centre of Kyoto counterculture favoured by leftists, photographers, and artists, including those visiting from the States like the poet Allen Ginsberg.

The Hite Report may have appealed especially to ūman ribu activists, for they, like Shere, saw sexuality as crucial to women's liberation. As scholar Setsu Shigematsu writes, 'the liberation of sex formed the core organizing logic of the movement'. This is present in the group's manifesto, penned by Tanaka Mitsu, one of the movement's key players; it called for 'liberation from the toilet'. As Mitsu theorised, women had been divided by a sexist society, either into 'Mother, maternal tenderness . . . an object to marry' or 'Toilet, the vessel to dispose of sexual urges'. In order to be seen as a mother, 'a woman has to act as though she sees nothing, hears nothing, and says nothing about sex, just like an innocent cute little girl'. Mitsu saw women as complicit in this, as they denied their own 'totality that possesses both tenderness' and 'natural sexual desire'. There is a radical openness in ūman ribu's theory of liberation. As Shigematsu puts it, it 'emphasiz[es] the creation of one's own practices of liberation' in the present 'and the open-endedness of what women may become in the future'.[11] It resembled *The Hite Report* in this way. Mitsu's manifesto concludes memorably, 'from woman to woman, from Toilet to Toilet! Unity Empowers Women! So are we gonna go for it?'[12]

Meeting Japanese feminists in person likely influenced Shere's understanding that there were lots of similarities between American and Japanese women when it came to sex. When asked by the media, she did not suggest that American women were further ahead, but stressed the similarities between these cultures. In both, the sexual gratification of men over women was prioritised. Shere told a journalist, 'There is a stereotype in Japan that American women are much more assertive and freer [than Japanese women]. And there are co-existing stereotypes in the United States about Japanese women . . . that they are submissive [but also] that Japanese society is more erotic than American society because we've all seen those prints', a reference to Shunga, or erotic woodblock art. Shere continued, 'I think the style is different in how American women express their feelings about what goes on in sex . . . but I've been hearing the same things here'.

What she does not say is that she and other American feminists had a lot to learn from Japanese feminists who understood that militarism and imperialism permeated sex too. In 'Liberation from the Toilet', Mitsu shared that the division of women into 'toilets' and 'mothers' explained the sexual enslavement of Korean women and girls to the Japanese forces during World War II—'the chastity of wives of the military nation and the dirtied pussies of the "comfort women" are the two extremes'—but this division impacted all women and their sex lives. While facing Japan's imperialist history, ūman ribu feminists were also hugely critical of the alliance between the United States and Japan and knew the United States would not save them. They were particularly critical of the treaty that allowed America to maintain military bases in Japan, which was forced on the Japanese as a condition of the end of the U.S. occupation. They described women as 'the greatest victim/greatest accomplice', a riff on Simone de Beauvoir, who wrote of women as 'half victim, half accomplice, like everyone'.[13] De Beauvoir's original meaning related only to women's role in maintaining sexism, wherein they are oppressed but also complicit. As citizens of a former imperialist power and fascist state, Japanese feminists also saw the complicity of women in imperialism. Shere could have learnt from them.

IN A VERY DIFFERENT CONTEXT, though one also affected by U.S. imperialism, *The Hite Report* was hugely popular in Brazil. When the book was published there, Brazil was under a right-wing military dictatorship that had taken power in a coup in 1964, with clandestine support from the United States. This deposed João Goulart, the social democratic president, and began a 'repressive and ferociously anti-communist' military government that led the country until 1985, the longest military dictatorship in South America.[14] These years were characterised by violence, torture, censorship, and the killing of dissidents in the name of state security. The regime promoted Christian family values and they justified their repression by appealing to women's 'innate commitment to family, morality, and social order'. Thousands of women heeded their call.[15] The most brutal years of the dictatorship between 1968 and 1974 were also the years of the so-called economic miracle, of massive growth from state-run projects and investment from U.S. and multinational companies. U.S. consumer goods became available and were desirable here. This was the stage *The Hite Report* stepped onto in Brazil.

Shere's book was translated into Portuguese by Karin Monika Winkler in 1978. Her Brazilian publishers heeded Shere's vision: no naked women graced the cover; no porny pictures were used to promote it. Shere was 'extremely happy with their handling of the book', and found Winkler's translation 'dignified and clear'. *The Hite Report* climbed quickly to number two on the Brazilian bestseller list. The book was a desirable commodity, symbolic of modernity. An unexpected source makes this clear. The Brazilian translation of *The Hite Report* appears in an advertisement for Levi's, a brand associated with young Americans that was first introduced to Brazil through members of the U.S. Peace Corps, emblematic of American soft power.[16] In the ad, a young woman is pictured in profile, curly hair partially obscuring her face, holding a copy of *O Relatório Hite*, along with a poster tube and Kodak photographic paper. She is dressed casually in an untucked button-down and Levi's, of course. She is utterly modern, and looks like a student, single and independent. Yet the caption chimes with the conservative morality of the regime, particularly regarding gender roles: 'If you know how to shop at the supermarket, have a coffee, take your child to school and on top of that wear Levi's . . . your future is secure, sweetheart'. The regime's reification of family values meant that even the most modern woman had to be a mother, and even a book like *The Hite Report* could be made to serve this vision.

Women from across the Southern Cone travelled to Brazil to buy *The Hite Report*, as it was banned in their own countries. One Argentine woman had travelled to Brazil and 'was able to find [the book] in English in São Paulo'. It was, she said 'one of the most important books I have ever read'. She wrote to Shere about the conditions of reading under a repressive regime: 'It seems strange to us, accustomed to living in a place where we are able to come in contact only with what morons decide is good for us, that there are other places where information of any kind if readily available. Here all information is mutilated either for religious or political or moral reasons. But we know that the real reason is stupidity'.

In the summer of 1978, *The Hite Report* was banned in Brazil. Police went into bookshops and confiscated it. Censorship was rife across the two decades of dictatorship; hundreds of novels, plays, music, films, and nonfiction books were censored in order to eliminate any left-wing influence that might threaten conservative values. The press was heavily censored, and articles were often pulled from publication at the last minute. To tip readers off about this, journalists sometimes replaced articles that had been pulled with cake recipes with unusual ingredients or pictures of demons.[17] The regime banned *The Hite Report* because it saw the family as the basis for upright morality in Brazil. Anything feminist or sexually explicit that challenged this was censored because according to officials this kind of material led 'to the downfall of families, of governments and the degradation of the nation as a whole'. It even increased Brazil's vulnerability to communism.[18] The book was banned for violating 'good and old customs'. 'Yes' wrote Shere 'the good and old custom of not having an orgasm'. The banning changed the meaning of book, from desirable commodity to anti-regime tract. Articles about *The Hite Report* were published in the press. Readers wrote in to agree with the ban: 'I've never seen such sophisticated filth disguised as well-meaning study'. *The Hite Report* made pornography 'seem as innocent as prayer books'. Others expressed their dismay at the ban: 'To censor a book like *The Hite Report* can only be the act of alienated and culturally primitive censors'. They made the point that the regime was allegedly liberalising politically and asked why this book based on women's testimony was banned 'as pornography', when actual porn was readily available on newsstands across the country.

Despite the ban, Shere went to Brazil in October 1978. The psychoanalytic community was particularly interested in her book and invited her as a guest speaker to their congress. Psychoanalysis boomed during the military dictatorship in Brazil. While the political landscape was repressive, more and more people, particularly the elites, took to the couch seeking personal release from inner tyranny. There is a flexibility to psychoanalysis. As we saw in chapter two, it can be a conservative force, depoliticising social problems and locating them in the individual. In Brazil, some therapists did conform with the regime. [19] But those in psychoanalytic circles who were interested in Shere's book were highly political and critical of it. They described the banning of the book as 'one of those surrealist things that happen all the time in this country', and were 'engaged in the campaign to obtain the revocation of this absurd measure'. They took seriously how psychoanalysis was inflected with politics and vice-versa. They thought about how therapy could go beyond 'a point of view identified with the elite' and beyond 'the consultation room, and [the] economically more privileged classes', to reach society as a whole. Reflective of their political stance, they asked Shere to speak on 'Sex as an institution', and they invited other speakers who, like Shere, questioned the politics of psychoanalysis, including French philosopher Félix Guattari, who was outspoken about the regime in Brazil. Karin Monika Winkler wrote to Shere as her visit approached, 'I hope you bring with you a great sunshine that can illuminate [and] enlighten the authorities in this country!'

Shere's publishers tried very hard to get the ban lifted, and they kept Shere updated through sending regular telegrams and letters, along with Brazilian coffee. Their first appeal was knocked back, and at Christmas of 1978, Winkler wrote to Shere, 'A nice present for all of us at this time would be, of course, having *The Hite Report* released. But unfortunately our Minister of Justice doesn't think so'. She urged, 'Let's not lose hope'. Pressure from feminists, leftists, and workers meant the regime had started to ease up on censorship. By August 1979, the book was back in circulation. Winkler phoned Shere, later writing to her: 'It was really nice talking to you again on the telephone the other day, specially because I could personally transmit to you the good news of having *The Hite Report* again in printing, after almost one year of having the book banned by the censor. I must say that this year, to me, seemed to be ten . . . I was waiting for this liberation and praying for it'. The only thing the censor changed, Winkler added, was to include a 'little remark' that 'the book is only recommended for adults. Let's now hope and pray that sales are like they were last year!' Winkler's prayers were answered, and in 1980 she sent a telegram to Shere: '*Hite Report* on No. one bestseller list, now in 9th printing'. She reported her total sales were 73,480, and that 'seldom book reaches this figure [in] Brasil'. By the end of 1980, the *Hite Report* was in its tenth printing.

Brazil, though, wasn't enough for Shere. She wanted the book to be published widely across the Global South, particularly in Africa and India. It is here that Shere's imperialist feminism can be seen, here that she acted most like the U.S. superhero come to save the women of the world. Like others in the U.S. women's movement at the time, she saw women coming from what was then called the Third World as 'behind' and in need of uplift by their American sisters. She wrote to her Australian publisher, Paul Hamlyn Books, who had the right to distribute the book to large swathes of the Global South, particularly former colonies of Britain in Asia and Africa. Paul Hamlyn Books didn't feel there was much of a market in these countries and was reluctant to publish. Shere urged them to create the market by publishing the book. She suggested women needed the book desperately. She wrote to them about India: 'The point of this letter is to remind you that I have not forgotten. I still want very much for the book to be distributed in India . . . My reason is that I think the women of India—and the men—could benefit greatly from my book. I wish I could make you understand how much it could mean to some people there, for health and happiness—so that you would rise above "business as usual" and think of the good you could do'.

In particular, Shere wanted her book to reach African women because of female genital cutting. Across the 1970s, some in the U.S. feminist movement became interested in this practice and associated it with Africa's Muslim populations. As *the* feminist who had brought the story of the clitoral orgasm to the mainstream and saw the potential of the clitoris for women's pleasure and liberation, Shere became outspoken on this issue. She came to know about female genital cutting through the work of Fran Hosken, an American feminist who had fled Hitler's Austria in 1938 and who coined the term 'female genital mutilation'. Hosken was outspoken about this practice in her newsletter *Women's International News* from 1972 onward. In 1979, when Shere was trying to get her book published globally, Fran Hosken wrote a controversial report about female genital cutting called *The Hosken Report*, very likely named after *The Hite Report*, which Hosken read carefully. This was based on her research in Africa, where she 'uncovered' the practice of female genital cutting. Hosken and Shere were also in touch.

The need for the book in places where female genital cutting was practiced became even clearer to Shere after Paul Hamlyn Books wrote to the Australian trade commissioner responsible for East Africa. The publisher enquired about whether there was a market for *The Hite Report* there. The trade commissioner replied that 'in the countries you are seeking a market, there is such a high rate of female circumcision and as such there is little or no importance attached to female sexuality except in terms of reproduction'. As Shere's book was 'an argument against the traditional female submissi[ve] sexual role', it 'would only appeal to the expatriate races and to a small percentage of the local population'. Shere wrote to Paul Hamlyn Books saying that she considered that letter 'a classic', demonstrative of how much women in these places needed her book and 'how badly some reform is needed'. To prove her point, she included some articles by Hosken.

Shere believed that violence against women occurred the world over, which it did then and continues to do. But Shere and Hosken set female genital cutting apart as the worst and most severe form of gendered violence. *The Hosken Report* described the 'genital and sexual mutilations of women to be the most drastic and physical form' of 'the crippling of women in a much broader sense'. Shere described it as evidence of 'an extremely negative view of women, a stage we in the West left behind centuries ago with the burning of "witches" in the Middle Ages'. Both saw this practice as evidence that African and Muslim cultures were inherently brutal and *more* patriarchal and violent than their own. Shere felt they were lagging 'behind' the West. As feminist Lila Abu-Lughod would put it, these feminists made female genital cutting into a form of 'spectacular cultural violence'. This kind of analysis of this practice encouraged a 'self-righteous commitment to change those backward or dysfunctional cultures'.[20] Hoskens and Shere also felt that African women were uniquely silenced and needed white feminists, along with their books and literature, to speak for them, modernise them and pull them forward in time. 'I am my sister's keeper', Hoskens wrote.[21]

Shere might have read some feminism coming out of Africa that was outspoken about all oppressive elements in the lives of women, including female genital cutting. She might have looked to Awa Thiam's work *Speak Out, Black Sisters* which came out of Senegal but for which Thiam interviewed a wide and diverse range of women from French-speaking Africa. First published in French in 1978 as *La Parole aux Négresses*, it has a strikingly similar methodology to *The Hite Report*. Thiam spoke to interviewed women about their whole lives, where they discuss 'happy and unhappy experiences: Black women's words and woes', when it came to love, family, work, marriage, and divorce.[22] Thiam, like Shere, used women's testimony as the basis for her analysis. Thiam and other African feminists like Malian Adi Gevins spoke out against female genital cutting but refused to see this as *distinct* from other forms of violence against women that took place globally. Similarly, Gevins undertook surveys on female genital cutting in French-speaking West Africa where 'she interviewed people and recorded some 200 songs on [female] circumcision' . . . which 'showed how our people express their norms, their rules, their educations'. They contextualised the practice not to explain it away but to understand it. They discussed female genital cutting politically, and refused to attribute it to the 'backwardness' of African Muslim cultures or to sensationalise it. Gevins commented on those campaigning against the practice from the United States, 'You know it is easy to see that something is wrong with the system when you are outside of it. Easier than when you are inside'.[23] The Association of African Women for Research and Development, based in Senegal, also released 'A Statement on Female Genital Mutilation' in 1980. They advocated for the total eradication of this practice but discussed how 'traditions [such as female genital cutting] with all of their constraints' become in contexts of colonisation and ensuing economic inequality 'a form of security for the peoples of the Third World'. They saw female genital cutting as a problem of politics, not culture, and suggested that white feminists' refusal to see this practice within the context of 'ignorance, obscurantism, exploitation and poverty', and their failure to question the structures and social relations that perpetuate the situation, was like 'refusing to see the sun in the middle of the day'.[24]

African feminists suggested that U.S. and European feminists campaigning against female genital cutting had reverted to imperialist feminism. The Association for African Women continued, stating Western feminists had 'forgotten . . .women from a different race and a different culture are also *human beings* . . .' and 'become insensitive to the dignity of the very women they want to save'. They had also forgotten the history of imperialism. Gevins wrote that while she was willing to use the work that westerners had done in her campaigning against female genital cutting, she wanted them understand, 'We have been colonised by this Western world . . . That means we don't want them to overwhelm our lives anymore . . . I want to collaborate with them. But I don't think I can be in the same group with them to fight something in my own country, because I will feel, "Here they go again, colonisation"'. She outlined an alternative to imperialist feminism for white and Black women working against female genital cutting. Their relations might be based in reciprocity and an ethics of 'suggestion' rather than imposition. 'Suggesting means that I can say no, or yes. That's different from "do that in Mali, do that in Senegal." I want them to allow me to say [to them], "I'm suggesting you do it this way, because these people are from my country and I think this will be better"'. Awa Thiam also challenged the schema underpinning imperialist feminism, which in Shere's case saw the United States as more advanced than Africa. Thiam wrote, 'The struggle of Black African woman can and must be conceived in some other way than as a carbon copy of the European woman's struggle'. But, she said, African women felt solidarity with all oppressed women of the world, as equals; 'whether that sisterhood is accepted or not, it is there'.

AT THE TIME, WOMEN DID write to Shere to contest the way that the book intended to speak to all the women in the world. A woman wrote from Italy, 'Your book is being sold in Italy. While I truly feel such a book should be available in Italy, I can't help feeling that it should be a book with questionnaires written by Italian women (likewise in other countries). Although women have a lot of common bonds, I think that culturally women of different countries would have different answers. I wonder how valid a book with the text by Americans is for . . . a society such as Italy'. Italian feminists wrote to the U.S. feminist periodical *Off Our Backs* and took issue with the way that *The Hite Report* was promoted in Italy as 'the latest, most scientific "American feminist" approach to sexuality', and the broader implication that Americans were more sexually advanced than other women or that they led the way in terms of feminism. Shere responded defensively. There is an unsigned letter published in *Off Our Backs* in support of Shere that she almost definitely wrote herself. She was upset that feminists had not given her the benefit of the doubt: 'Why can't you imagine that I might have undergone severe agitation and anxiety over my lack of control of the publication of these books around the world . . . Did it never occur to you that I might be suffering, and fighting and working every minute of the day and night, seven days a week . . . trying to save, convince and improve . . . all the editions'. Radical feminist Andrea Dworkin wrote a letter on Shere's behalf to this magazine too. She suggested that the Italian woman were intimating that 'a woman from the United States [is] insensitive to economic issues because of her nation of birth and acculturation. The anger here is misdirected, an ally is named as an enemy'. She ends with a hyperbolic statement, a style she is known for: 'I cannot bear to see her work discredited and the smirk on the rapist's face'.

Others around the world productively used *The Hite Report* as a point of departure for their own studies, reinterpreting the book locally to make it meaningful. Shere received letters from keen amateur and professional researchers informing her that they would begin their own studies, as well as an invitation to do some joint research comparing Puerto Rican women to those in the rest of the United States. Sonia Cuales, UN coordinator for women's affairs in the Caribbean, wrote that she would like to disseminate the questionnaires to women in the region as the basis for a study, though she might make some changes: 'A number of [questions] are applicable to women all over the world', though 'many of the questions relate specifically to the North American cultural context'. A professor dropped Shere a line from the Philippines. He had used *The Hite Report* in a graduate course on human sexuality: 'The Filipino women really related to it and my graduate students are now replicating your study for the Third World woman which will open up a whole new area in female psychology'. His study began with 'Filipinas have never been asked how they feel about sex'.[25]

These criticisms led Shere to include a tear-out sheet in the back of all the foreign editions. Across eight questions, women could write to her about how they felt about the book. She asked women what they agreed and disagreed with, and 'What would you like to add that is unique to your country? Are there other topics that are important for your country?' This was as far as she went. Some white U.S. feminists came to understand that their feminism was tainted with imperialism by taking Black and Latin American feminism seriously. Adrienne Rich wrote that there were 'problems and dangers of seeing our particular issues as some kind of model or vanguard for women everywhere . . . a common North American, Euro American, form of chauvinism'.[26] Unfortunately, Shere was not able to see things this way. For her, as for some others, this sense that American feminists were ahead, and that specific cultures were inherently oppressive to women, developed into a full-blown Islamophobic feminism in the 1990s. Shere wrote articles celebrating the 'secular' values of the west, describing the chador as a 'slave-like uniform', and comparing Islamic states with Nazi Germany. She defended the role of the United States in the First Gulf War, 'which for many people, was a war against Islam'. She asked rhetorically, 'Do we in the West have the right to tell Arab women that part of their culture is wrong, that they are oppressed? Don't many Arab women say that they prefer to live as they do? Yes, but so did our grandmothers last century'. So, in her mind, the West was indeed justified. She was certainly not alone here, and we see this logic at play in the feminist justification for recent wars and conflict. The invasion of Afghanistan in 2001 is a premier example, presented as necessary to liberate Muslim women from the Taliban. This was praised as a 'restoration of hope' by Hillary Clinton and a 'coalition of hope' by *Ms.* magazine.[27] But the invasion was opposed by grassroots feminists in Afghanistan, including the oldest feminist group in the country, the Revolutionary Association of the Women of Afghanistan. While outspoken against the oppressive fundamentalism of the Taliban, RAWA called for it to be 'overthrown by the uprising of the Afghan nation', not U.S. invasion, which would 'shed the blood of numerous women, men, children, young and old of our country', which it did.[28]

It is a shame that Shere went this way, because her imperialist feminism made solidarity and reciprocity with Global South feminists impossible. But also because her fantasy of a liberated, secular United States located the most severe forms of gender injustice beyond it. This did not equip her to understand what was happening to her when she was subject to religious-inspired New Right backlash in the late 1980s and 1990s, which I discuss in the next chapters.

CHAPTER 5
MEN: LEFT, RIGHT, AND LEFT BEHIND

In 1977, a man working on a drilling rig in Alaska, far from home, sat down and wrote to Shere Hite. After a day of work as a 'roughneck', a physically demanding job handling the drill in freezing Arctic conditions, I imagine he washed the oil and mud off, made a coffee, lit a cigarette, borrowed a typewriter, and wrote to Shere in fits and starts, the lines irregular, the spaces erratic. After two days of reading *The Hite Report* wherever he could, in the back of the rec room, lying on his bunk in close quarters with other men, he had reached page 383 and begun his letter. 'My wife gave me your book to read . . . My first reaction was "What is my wife trying to tell me?" I promised my wife I would read your book and it has been one of the best promises I have ever kept. Your book has been a mind opener. Until reading your book I felt I was a great lover and all around good guy . . . With the honesty of the various women, I have found my shortcomings . . . Maybe your book is my wife's way of communicating with me, at least opening the door'.

There are thousands and thousands of letters from men in the archive; half the responses Shere received about *The Hite Report* were from male readers across the United States. Like the letters from 'normal' women, and the global reception of the book, men's responses to *The Hite Report* revise our feminist storylines. The story usually goes that most men were not touched by the women's liberation movement at all, that it did not change them. 'No huge crowds of men have become feminists', wrote Raewyn Connell, theorist of masculinity.[1] Michael Messner goes further, saying, 'Most men responded with either hostility or stunned silence to the women's liberation movement'.[2] Men's responses to *The Hite Report* show that feminism did reach men. They had complex and difficult feelings about it, they wondered and worried how they could be men in the wake of this movement, and sometimes they changed. In contrast, men's responses to Shere's next book, *The Hite Report on Male Sexuality* published in 1981, demonstrate how in a few short years, men's knotty feelings calcified into anti-feminism as the storm clouds of the backlash gathered on the horizon.

When *The Hite Report* first came out, how women should relate to men was a huge question for feminists. The women's liberation movement had developed from the New Left, particularly the movement against the Vietnam War, which was saturated with sexism. Women printed the leaflets and made the coffee while men stood on the platform and made the speeches. When women made their case for 'full participation in all aspects of movement work', they were laughed off the stage, catcalled, told to 'cool down' and shut up.[3] An organising culture that refused to see them as equals left women with little choice but to organise alone. They were also inspired by the Black Power movement, which posed that those who faced a particular oppression should be the ones who devised the solutions and organised against it.[4] Shere believed in the importance of women-only groups and benefited from the way these helped women to imagine themselves differently and develop their own identity beyond men. Through organising together, women learnt to see each other as interesting, clever, and admirable, not just people to compete with for male attention. But Shere never gave up on men. She understood that men were trapped by sexism too and had a role to play in gender justice. In the last pages of *The Hite Report*, she mused, 'Isn't it possible that men have been told "mounting and thrusting" is the "right" thing to do, but they too, if allowed to experiment, would find many other ways they liked to have intercourse?' She concluded, 'Men can profit by opening up and re-examining their conception of sexuality'. If men would do so, sex might become more 'androgynous'. She began a project on male sexuality and encouraged male readers to write her for a survey and they did, in droves.

Shere's position on men was influenced by the men's liberation movement, a small group of anti-sexist men who supported feminism. These men were mostly educated, white, middle-class, and outspoken about women's oppression. They organised demonstrations, including against *Playboy*, where they chanted, 'One, two, three, four, we don't want *Playboy* anymore. Five, six, seven, eight, smash the image, smash the state'.[5] They ran crèches so that women could talk and do politics. These men argued that patriarchy injured men too. [6] Aspiring to be 'real men' made men lonely, emotionally repressed, and scared to get close to others, particularly other men. In the first *Hite Report*, Shere drew on Marc Feigen Fasteau's men's liberation text, *The Male Machine*. Feigen Fasteau argued that the masculine ideal made men into robots, 'programmed to tackle jobs, attack problems, and always seize the offensive'.[7] The so-called ideal man 'wields his authority over [women] effortlessly', reminding them of 'his superior design' and quashing rebellion through an 'awe-inspiring flex of mechanical muscle'. Feigen Fasteau's book stresses that the obsession with male orgasm combined with the 'masculine disdain for feeling makes it hard for men to grasp that the state of desire is the best part'. Shere agreed.

Marc Feigen Fasteau worked closely with Warren Farrell, who wrote the U.S. 'bible' of the anti-sexist men's movement, *The Liberated Man*. Farrell served three terms on the NOW board of directors, set up male consciousness-raising groups around the country, and organised beauty contests where men were judged in their underwear so they could feel how it was to be a sex object. Farrell was often referred to as the leader of the men's movement in glowing reportage that showed him whipping up a breakfast omelette for his wife. He creatively suggested gender-neutral 'human vocabulary', including gender-neutral pronouns te/tir and 'attaché', meaning 'a person with whom one had a deep emotional attachment', as an alternative to husband/wife. He, like Shere and Feigen Fasteau, felt that when it came to sex, men needed 'sensuality training', akin to assertiveness training for women. Men would learn 'to be comfortable with women in control' during sex and help them 'appreciate the total sensual experience', not just male orgasm.[8]

A FEW MEN'S LIBERATIONISTS SENT letters to Shere. One wrote on paper headed 'every woman a wonder woman'. One is from a serious anti-rape activist, who wrote 'really dig what you are doing'. Another wrote of his intention to discuss the book at his men's CR group. He signed off 'in struggle', the letter decorated with a drawing of his collective house, a rainbow coming out of the chimney. I can almost smell the lentil soup simmering on the stove. Not all feminists agreed with Shere about the role men could play. They were often sceptical of anti-sexist men whose commitment to the movement could be shallow.

As Warren Farrell wrote, 'men tend to stand up and give speeches, they dominate small discussion groups . . . they solve problems rather than ask questions'. One letter read like a satire of a feminist man. He told Shere he was the 'only man ever invited to read poetry' at a women's liberation meeting; 'I read my long poem (11 minutes)', which was about how he enlightened his female friend who was 'very oppressed' about Betty Friedan.

For Shere, the 'man' question was not just political. She was a bisexual woman and passionate lover of men. She remained enthralled with the idea of romance, of being swept off her feet. These fantasies are notoriously hard to shake, even for the most committed feminist, because of the bombardment of images of the woman in love who shapeshifts into 'slave, queen, flower, doe, stained-glass window, doormat, servant, courtesan, muse, companion . . . depending on the lover's fleeting dreams', as Simone de Beauvoir wrote.[9] Joanna Briscoe, Shere's partner in the 1990s, described how both her family life and the era she grew up in had primed Shere to find men all too interesting. She sometimes remained quite beholden to men and would act as if they were the most important people in the room. As we have seen, she grew up poor, at a time when marriage was the only socially sanctioned future for a woman like her. Perhaps the abandonments of her early life meant she held on tightly to dreams of being rescued. Shere had relationships and affairs across her life and sought out partners, including through a dating service for classical music lovers where she used the nom de plume Diana Gregory.

In the archive there are some notes titled 'Times I loved' that read like scenes from a romantic film. These include going on a date to a romantic restaurant and 'driving back looking at the moon—it was huge, gold and round'. And 'Once you said y[ou] wished we had known each other for a long, long time'. There is a letter to a lover who is named only as 'Darling' that she wrote on the plane, 'so I wouldn't forget ever' your 'brown eyes like orbs', your 'shoulders and strength. I love when you hold me'. A fan of the grand gesture, she imagined 'jumping up and leaving the plane' and rushing home to them. She wrote of their sexual passion: 'I love it when you give me an O[rgasm]. Or when you were on top and came and came . . . and told me you had fantasised about marrying me'. Her romantic engagements put her at odds with some feminists. In the 1970s, parts of the movement questioned heterosexual romance and sex for the way it reinforced and rewarded women's dependence on men. Feminists suggested celibacy, not because women should deny themselves pleasure but to get their lives back and get to know themselves rather than spending their precious time pouring themselves into relationships with men. Later, vocal parts of the movement advocated for political lesbianism. Women should channel their desire, their passion, their love, their admiration and interest, which they usually reserved for men, into women. Women could change who the love object was.[10] Shere did not feel that women needed to be set free from wanting heterosexual love and sex entirely but that these institutions needed to become equal and more pleasurable to become worthy of women's desire.

Shere expressed interest in men during her hundreds of media appearances, including in magazines such as *Playboy* and *Penthouse*. This helped her take feminism far beyond its usual sphere to all kinds of men. *The Hite Report* was the first feminist book many men read, and sometimes it was the last. Indicative of Shere's wide reach is a collection of extraordinary letters from incarcerated men who found out about Shere from porn. In their letters they discussed their hopes for life afterward, including love and sex. They provide a stark contrast to the idea of prisoners as invulnerable, violent, and hypermasculine: 'I am single, 30 years old . . . I am at the present time in [jail] for burgling a dwelling. I got ten years for it in 1968 and I will discharge in 19 more months. I'm half American Indian, one quarter French Canadian. When I am free, I travel the rodeo circuit and am on the road all the time unless I'm minding some broken bones . . . which I have done a few times . . .' This man agreed with Shere's perspective on sex: 'I hear complaints from dudes like "man, all she did was lay there and no action" and my first thought was that this dude was probably the one who didn't know what he was doing'. Others wrote to praise the book's focus on female pleasure: 'I have been delegated by 7 other prisoners at the Kansas State Industrial Reformatory to write this letter. We have all finished reading your questionnaire in the March issue of *Penthouse*. Due to the excellent . . . report on female sexuality, we know that your upcoming book on the male side will be terrific. So we say "Right on Shere Hite. Right the Hell on"'.

Men loved *The Hite Report* because it taught them how to be better lovers. Across the United States, women thrust the book into their lovers' and husbands' hands. Often women felt unable to start a conversation about sex themselves, so the book worked as a proxy. Men wrote to Shere about where they found out about sex before her book. Working-class men got information from other men, workmates, and brothers: 'the B.S. stuff you heard behind the garage or in the gym'. One man had 'learned [about sex] from whores around the world'. Middle-class men were more likely to have read Freud, Kinsey, and Masters and Johnson. A doctor wrote to tell Shere that 'in all my years of medical training I have yet to read a book which gives us such a full blown dose of information and gut honesty as your book does'. Many men learnt about sex from porn, which, as Shere said in an interview, 'tells men to keep going as they are'. Compared to the usual sources of sexual knowledge, a man described *The Hite Report* as 'a bright light in darkness that has existed for too long'. Men thought the book should be compulsory reading, that every home in the United States should have a copy. They suggested Shere develop it into a marriage manual or a textbook for teenagers taught in school. Men's sex lives improved after reading the book, and some became evangelical about *The Hite Report*: 'I find myself being forced . . . to tell my friends of both sexes to "read the damned book!"' A dispatcher for a taxi company propped the book up on his desk as he worked the phones and assigned the jobs. He saw this as a public service announcement: 'Lots of cab drivers have lots to learn as you probably have experienced'.

Shere's beauty made her message more palatable. In prison in Utah, a man wrote, 'I was mesmerized at your beauty and also your intent of displaying truth about sexual intimacy'. A childcare worker who dabbled in astrology in Berkeley sent a picture in response to her own in the paper, as if she had placed it there for him, personally. He asked her out, and he is not alone there. Men wrote: 'If you're ever in San Francisco', 'If you're ever in Atlanta', 'If you're ever in Detroit and need a friend'. Some men misinterpreted Shere's beauty, her candid discussion of sex and interest in men, as an invitation. Her beauty was viewed as a promise: *Read my book and you'll get to date—maybe even fuck—women like me.* There are a small number of toe-curlingly sleazy and violently threatening letters in the archive. A racquetball instructor on stationery decorated with sports equipment wrote, 'glad that I obtained your trash report from our local library since the asking price is such a rip off . . . just like the fem side you presented in this nonsense you call a . . . study of female sexuality'. He ends the letter with a slimy invitation: 'Should you find yourself in Chicago feel free to call me for a lesson or two about sexuality and racquetball'. He signed off, his name followed by 'PhD', which he underlined. A night shift worker invited Shere: 'Shall we make love?' His tone is coy—'You sure you're not afraid of my dragons? If you come to me you're going to encounter them?'—but smut oozes everywhere as he signs off: 'May I play with your breasts and suck them?' One man relished composing a long, obscene list of all the ways *The Hite Report* made men superfluous. Women 'just want to fuck a candle or bottle or a large broom handle'. Several men brag about penis size and send drawings. One described his huge cock as 'impressive in its very veiny and gnarled hardness'; he signs off anonymously as 'a well-hung reader', the coward. There is one letter from an incarcerated man in which he shares racialised rape fantasies. At least he signed off with his name. Shere wrote on the envelope, 'If this is a product of our society and prisons—I am worried for us all'. She replied to these letters the same way she replied to all mail from men: She sent them the male sexuality questionnaire.

The Hite Report hooked men in because it taught them how to have sex with women. But this was not just a sexual self-help book, it was not *The Joy of Sex*; feminism lay at its heart. While women found the book clarifying and relieving, male readers found its feminism profoundly disorienting. Their letters to Shere overflow with complex feelings, speaking against expectations that men practice emotional restraint. Many men began their letters by listing the range of emotions that flooded through them and into each other as they digested the book and its findings: 'I became alternately horrified, sad, angry, and amused at the ladies' answers'. 'At various times I felt angry (scapegoated) guilt, understood, hopeful and excited'. Men's responses, then, were much more emotionally chaotic than women's. While women went from not knowing to knowing, like turning up the contrast dial on a television screen, for men, the picture became blurred. They often finished reading plagued by a sense that they did not know why they behaved as they did. 'I've always enjoyed the preliminaries much more than the main event in sex. And yet I've always felt a need to rush as quickly as possible to the actual act of intercourse . . . Why, I don't honest-to-god know'. Another man was deeply sad: 'I ask myself why I have not changed, I do not know. I think it is a fear of rejection; but why I think I would be rejected, I do not know'. *The Hite Report* was a particularly painful read when it contradicted how men saw themselves: 'I think you have altered the rest of my life . . . Could it be true that I had . . . been conceited enough to believe I was being a complete . . . sexual partner? Was I too enmeshed in that trap of maleness that I despise?'

In their letters, men open up to the possibility of feminism, double down, and open up again, oscillating wildly between solidarity and oppression. One man began (and this is quite typical), 'Your work on human sexuality is superb', but then added, 'Literally hundreds of times, I wanted to correct what I felt I were erroneous assumptions by women contributors . . .' There is a stack of 'not all men' letters. As they see it, the women's testimonies are interesting, but don't apply to them because of their outstanding sexual prowess. The most lively of these is from 'an ex Gigilo [*sic*]' who had 'dated women of all ages, nationality, shape, sizes from midgets to 400 Lb gals, I have also had as many as five dates in one evening, and after dating hundreds of women, I have yet to get one complaint from any woman, I've always guaranteed sexual fulfilment . . .' Perhaps of the stack, this was the letter most likely to be true, given that this man was having sex for money.

In a stark example, a man began his letter full of anger: 'I finished *The Hite Report* two minutes ago. I saw myself described on its pages so many times by your uncommunicative anonymous respondents that I partly want to help get our side of [it] heard . . . I hope you got some input from a few hairy beasts (adult males to you, you libber)'. Shere has struck through this in green several times. But, then he included a P.S., which she circled with ticks and stars: 'All kidding to the side, please accept my deep and awed congratulations on your undertaking and accomplishment so far'.

Men's confusion reflected their feelings about feminism more broadly. The women's movement seemed to have upended everything, and they were left feeling winded in its wake. Relationships and sexual expectations changed at the same time that many states transitioned to no-fault divorce laws, which made it easier to end a marriage. Journalists told Shere in interviews that feminism had brought 'pain and confusion' when it came to dating: 'There doesn't seem any nice Victorian protocol you can follow, it is very hard for people to grope their way'. Men felt the change at work too; across the 1970s, women entered the workforce in record numbers due to the women's movement and the culmination of an upward trend since World War II. More single, divorced, and widowed women worked outside the home than ever before, and by 1975 nearly half of all married women did too.[11] Women began to break into all-male bastions of work. There were female firefighters, surgeons, scientists, and engineers, plus laws to protect them from being harassed out of the job. *Time* magazine celebrated this in 1976, the year the first *Hite Report* came out. They declared that feminism had 'transcended the feminist movement . . . to a new status of general—and sometimes unconscious—acceptance'.[12] But men weren't so sure. Two years earlier, in 1974, recession had struck. Unemployment was at the highest level recorded since the end of World War II, and workers in blue-collar industries like manufacturing and construction suffered acutely.[13] While deindustrialisation and recession were due to global economic shifts, including the oil crisis of 1973, they coincided with the women's movement, and men wondered if they were losing their jobs because of this. Women in the workplace were, after all, much more visible and closer at hand than the faraway events that caused the recession. Feminism didn't quell men's uncertainty and scepticism. It focussed on women, and it didn't discuss what feminism could do for men or suggest how they might negotiate these sweeping changes. As feminist bell hooks wrote, feminism did not offer 'guidelines and strategies for alternative masculinity'; it did not offer a blueprint.[14]

I read these letters by men going back and forth, giving up power and claiming it back, and was also reminded of the way that white women too, many of us feminists, equivocate as we are asked to give up power to align with people of colour. Within the history of feminism are many examples of white women similarly pirouetting between solidarity and oppression; we cry, we deny our own racism, we feel bad, we are sorry then claim innocence, we direct our anger at the wrong people, often the very people we have harmed.[15] Or, like these men, we want to discuss our complex, rocky process with those we have oppressed and we expect them to listen. This can be tough on people. One woman described how 'she found herself reacting with mixed emotions' as her partner expressed 'huge guilt feelings' about all his relationships after reading *The Hite Report*. She'd been trying to tell him the same thing for years, so she felt disappointed and angry.

While trying to rid themselves of sexism, perhaps men shouldn't have talked about how difficult this was for them with women, including their partners and Shere. But these letters are more honest than those from men who wrote to tell Shere that they didn't find the transformation difficult *at all*. They told Shere how easy it was, to make themselves look good in her eyes. This is what the Black scholar-activist Nova Reid calls, in the context of white people unlearning racism, 'performative allyship'. It is trying to do 'anti-racism work while remaining comfortable, to actively avoid confronting feelings which is just not possible'.[16]

When men did change, it was because they felt the power of the women's movement. The woman who listened to her husband's guilt reported that only 'now that several thousand women were saying the same thing, he accepted my feelings as valid'. This was a bitter pill to swallow, but it also shows us how effective social movements work. This woman's words were echoed by the thousands of women in *The Hite Report*, and so he took notice. Men also changed when they realised unlearning sexism would benefit them. One man wrote that he learnt of 'the monumental insensitivity and lack of gentleness and caring women have suffered . . . at the hands of man.' But he had also realised that 'I can be freed, along with my sisters'.

While the book helped men become better and more feminist lovers, it didn't tell them how to be better men, so those who were putting these actions into practice described feelings of uncertainty and fear as well as great determination: 'I'm frightened because I don't know how . . . [but] Your work has set the wheels in motion for a desire to break away from predictable patterns of action and thought'. Another wrote, 'This has been incredible. You are incredible. The only suitable thank you . . . is to try to develop my own support systems for real, humane, vulnerable, aware contact. In an insane society, this is a project of years, not weeks. But the way is open, and my bags are packed'. As a feminist book, *The Hite Report* offered a way for men to get back parts of themselves they had lost. As one man wrote plainly, 'I think men need your book in order to become more fully human themselves'.

Men's letters would have buoyed Shere. They suggested that her project on male sexuality was much needed, so she got on with it. Shere collected and analysed questionnaires from seven thousand men. Unlike the first book, *The Hite Report on Male Sexuality* went far beyond sex to ask men about their relationships, about love, and about being a man, across 168 questions. She asked about sexual preferences, desires, and orgasm, of course, but also: 'What was the happiest you ever were with someone?' 'When were you the loneliest?' 'How would you define masculinity?' On *The Larry King Show*, she described her methodology: 'In the beginning I distributed questionnaires in batches. I would mail to clubs, I would mail bulk mailings with a cover letter to the club president—it could be a university men's club, it could be something like Kiwanis, it could be a senior citizens club . . . as many clubs as I could find', all across the United States. She then checked her distribution against the U.S. population and targeted populations she didn't have enough of, including specific geographical areas and ages. The methodology is an improvement on the first *Hite Report*.

She delivered a three-foot-tall manuscript to Robert Gottlieb, her editor at Knopf. He cut and shaped it, but it still stretched to over 1,100 pages, mostly men speaking about their own lives. Her top-line findings for this project were that most men didn't marry the woman they most passionately loved. Men were 'proud of that', she reported. 'They thought they should be rational, that when it came to choosing a marriage partner you shouldn't let your feelings carry you away'. When asked who their best friend was, most men said their wife, and most felt male friendships lacked emotional closeness. She also found that 72 percent of men in long-term relationships had affairs. She hastened to add that the book was not about the statistics but the conversations between real people, who she quotes at length and who 'debate with each other how to live their lives'.

The most interesting and new thing about *The Hite Report on Male*

Sexuality was the range of men who discussed how difficult it was to live up to standards of masculinity. Men discussed how ideal masculinity subordinated women but also created a hierarchy among men. This would later be called 'hegemonic masculinity' by Raewyn Connell and was key to masculinity studies in the late 1980s and 1990s, but men discuss it here. Men who were deemed not to measure up to standards of masculinity as boys talked about being shamed and called 'sissies' by fathers, older brothers, and friends. Men described the pressure of striving for this unreachable standard: 'Men are trained at an early age to disregard any and every emotion and *be strong*. You take someone like that and you wonder why they don't . . . can't express feelings . . . They are supposed to be a cross between John Wayne, the Chase Manhattan Bank and Huge Hefner. We are only human for Christ sake'. This resonated with readers, and Shere got some letters from men about this book. She and her ex-boyfriend Martin Sage went out to dinner to read them. Sage recalled the surreal moment: 'We sat in a very quaint Czechoslovakian restaurant on the Upper East Side . . . looking over the responses . . . surrounded by émigrés from Czechoslovakia, eating Wiener schnitzel'. One man who really liked the book gushed: 'I want to thank you personally. Five times when I was reading I stopped and whispered "I love you Shere"'. A photographer's assistant found a 'statement made by the handicapped man' in the book 'very moving and very truthful because I have Cerebral Palsy . . . Most people would say I am doing better than some other black men my age who are either unemployed, in jail, or in their graves. But some of them have what I want, a serious female relationship'. Resonant with the disabled woman in chapter three, he added, 'I wish you would do an in-depth study and report on the problems of sexuality and the disabled, it would help a lot'.

The letters weren't plentiful, and the book wasn't lauded like the first *Hite Report*. While 125,000 copies were printed, it didn't fly off the shelves. The reviews were mixed. Women reporters wrote it up positively. Lynn Langway writing for *Newsweek* called it a 'riveting document that strips away many of the most cherished—and destructive—myths about sexuality'. In contrast, many male interviewers were angry or defensive. On the talk show *Leave It to the Women*, Shere faced a panel of male daytime TV actors. She suggested that it was difficult for men to speak about how masculinity made them unhappy. The actor Gil Gerard came out swinging and proved her point through his vehement denial: 'I don't agree with that at all, that's never been true of anyone I've ever known . . .' Later in the interview, faced with men's unhappiness in the book, he said, 'You cannot use one man's torment as a yardstick to measure other men with'. Shere suggested that she wasn't 'trying to "measure" men but simply stage a conversation so men could make up their own minds'. Measure, she noted, 'was a very male word'. Historically, men's measurement of sexual behaviour had left out the important domain of feelings, which she was interested in. Gerard talked over her: 'What about measure a cup of sugar, measure a tablespoon of something?' Shere was shocked by men's responses. She told Larry King, 'I was very surprised. I thought this book wasn't as controversial [as the first *Hite Report*]. I thought this book was very sympathetic to men . . . it didn't occur to me that this book would arouse so much controversy as it had'.

BY 1981, THE TEMPEST AGAINST feminism was rolling in. In 1979, the country had once again fallen into recession because of an oil crisis, this time caused by the Iranian Revolution. Further, 1980 was, as journalist Susan Faludi wrote, 'a moment of symbolic crossover [between] men and women: the first time white men became less than 50 percent of the work force, the first time more women than men enrolled in college . . . the first time more than 50 percent of married women worked, the first time the U.S. Census stopped defining the head of the household as the husband'. And the first time no new manufacturing jobs were created.[17] By now, there were many seductive anti-feminist explanations for men to channel their feelings of confusion and precarity into. These appealed to men who weren't sure how to act in light of feminism. Complex feelings of uncertainty that men had expressed to Shere after reading the first *Hite Report* hardened into hostility and a sense of grievance that men were losing out and feminism was to blame.

The worst write-up of *The Hite Report on Male Sexuality* was from Philip Nobile in *New York Magazine*. He used biology to excuse sexism. This influenced how the book was reviewed more widely, with many critics parroting his position. Nobile argued that Shere 'whipped herself up into an antipatriarchal frenzy', and as a result the book was a 'travesty of sex research'. Her science was bad and flawed not because of her methodology, but because she didn't understand the fundamental 'natural' differences between men and women. She 'harp[ed] on about the cultural imperatives of intercourse [and so] totally neglects biology—as if genes had nothing to do with our own sexual predicament'. He disagreed with her use of feminist prehistory too. She suggested, as in the first *Hite Report*, that before Christ 'the sexual behaviour of . . . societies was much more diverse and less coitus-oriented'. In contrast, Nobile used prehistory to argue that 'intercourse everywhere is the *sin qua non*', the essential condition, 'of sex'. Men were, and always had been, naturally promiscuous, they wanted to sow their seed and have as many babies as possible. These 'dispositions evolved over millions of years because they promoted reproductive success'. Other reviews argued this too; there was a real pessimism in the way they reduced men to their 'biological' urges. Shere noted: 'If I were a man I would rather think that my behaviour wasn't ruled by hormones . . . that I wasn't "a beast" or "a caveman"'. But this did get men off the hook. Men were beholden to nature. There was nothing they could do about it. They did not need to grapple with complex feelings about feminism or try to change; that was just denying biology, or even punishing them for what they could not control. Some men's responses to *The Hite Report on Male Sexuality* reflected this: 'Please don't try to change us. It isn't wrong for a man to be strong, self-confident and relatively unemotional. It's just the way some men are'.

Nobile waged a personal war against Shere. He published a column in the *SoHo Weekly News* under the pseudonym V. de Foggia called 'Eight Bitchy Questions for Shere Hite'. Question one asked Shere whether her 'postgraduate work in porn modelling might have twisted your feelings toward men and . . . biased your research?' Shere sued him for $15 million. Nobile said 'he stood by every comma', so she appointed none other than Roy Cohn as her lawyer. Cohn was a notoriously aggressive lawyer to the stars, the mob, and the Catholic church, a supporter of Ronald Reagan, hugely corrupt, and a closeted gay homophobe. Cohn built his reputation assisting Joseph McCarthy's investigation into suspected communists in the 1950s. He sent Ethel and Julius Rosenberg to their deaths for Soviet espionage. He is also the man who made Donald Trump. In 1973, he provided counsel when the Trump real estate company was being sued by the federal government for racial discrimination. Cohn got them off the charges and became a mentor to Trump, teaching him 'the Roy Cohn playbook': Never admit defeat, fight back, fight dirty, and claim victory.[18] Shere likely employed Cohn because it meant the case would get press. They settled out of court and Shere wrote to Cohn, who was by then very sick with AIDS, 'Dear Roy, To say I am elated at . . . your success in the matter of my lawsuit . . . would certainly be an understatement. I feel like a different person and I have the energy to continue my life'.

Even notorious 'attack dog' Roy Cohn couldn't protect Shere. By the 1980s, the idea that sexism was due to 'natural' differences between men and women was everywhere. It was particularly favoured by the the New Right, a grassroots coalition of right-wing groups. They entangled biblical and scientific explanations to uphold gender hierarchy. Historians suggest that the New Right became a force to be reckoned with in 1976, the year the first *Hite Report* was published. Conservative Christian Americans found the upheavals of the 1960s to be a shattering of their worlds. Women's liberation and civil rights had changed cultural and sexual norms, and they found themselves out of step. Many people felt frozen out, 'an embattled faithful remnant' against the entirety of American society, whose morals had fallen off a cliff into the cold sea.[19] The New Right organized this discontent. Evangelical leaders, including Jerry Falwell and Tim LaHaye, rallied their troops and began to speak out against feminism as part of the vast web of liberal interests that had ensnared the United States, promoting abortion, gay rights, government meddling in private affairs, the shrinking of the military, increased taxes, and compulsory desegregation.

Initially, the backlash was fought on the terrain of race, but by the end of the 1960s, when expressions of overt white supremacy became politically toxic, they set their guns on feminism. In 1980, Falwell published his bestselling polemic *Listen, America!* In this screed, he mixed biology with the Bible to declare that 'feminists live in disobedience to God's laws and have promoted their godless philosophy throughout our society. God Almighty created men and women biologically different and with differing needs and roles. He made men and women to complement each other and to love each other. [Women] need to be part of a home where their husband is a godly leader and where there is a Christian family'.[20] One man who had previously been part of the radical left wrote to Shere about finding God. This resolved his confusion about feminism: 'So much changed when I finally admitted I couldn't make it alone . . . In an interview you said you were from a "bible-belt" background. I don't know how you feel about Jesus, but speaking for myself, I know he has changed my heart'.

Right-wing women also got in on the act. Male evangelical leaders needed women to smooth their rough edges and prove that they were not just a bunch of aggrieved white men. These women had been organising since the early 1970s, but 1976 was the year right-wing women *got* organised. Phyllis Schlafly, a gifted political leader and right-wing Catholic, led the successful campaign against the Equal Rights Amendment. By 1976, her group, the Eagle Forum, was larger than NOW. That same year, Anita Bryant, conservative Southern Baptist, ambassador for Florida orange juice, and singer, began her campaign to 'Protect America's Children' against gay rights. In 1976, the Hyde Amendment was brought in, which restricted the use of public funds for abortion, making it more difficult for women, especially poor, often racialised women, to access. This was an early victory for a growing movement. In 1977, a coalition of feminists led by Bella Abzug held the National Women's Conference in Houston. This was the largest, most dynamic, and most diverse feminist conference held in U.S. history. But, as historian Marjorie Spruill has discussed, right-wing women held their own fifteen-thousand-strong Pro-Life, Pro-Family rally close by and staged interventions at the feminist conference. These women described Houston as 'their bootcamp'. Republican strategists learnt from these women. It was because of the efforts of right-wing women that Republicans centred anti-feminism and gender and sexuality in their electoral platform alongside economic conservativism and national defence in 1980. Reagan's landslide owed a lot to them.[21]

Right-wing women published books that used biology to make the argument for rigid hierarchical gender roles. Their books sold tens of thousands of copies in Christian and right-leaning circles. Phyllis Schlafly wrote that biological sex differences between men and women were naturally reflected in different sexual priorities: 'the man is orgasm-oriented' while the woman is 'engulfed in romanticism'.[22] These women also ushered in a Christian sexual revolution. Within a marriage based on rigid gender roles and wifely submission, sex could be hot and holy. There was no need for Christian couples to limit themselves to the missionary position. Marabel Morgan counselled wives to spice it up in her Evangelical self-help book *The Total Woman*. They might wait at the door when their husbands arrived home from work in an outrageously sexy outfit (think showgirl or cowgirl, or—her most famous suggestion—greeting him wearing only cling wrap). New Right leaders Beverley and Tim LaHaye integrated Shere's finding about the need for clitoral stimulation into their Christian sex handbook, *The Act of Marriage*. The LaHayes talked explicitly about 'the clitoris which must be stimulated . . . for the wife to achieve orgasm'. They interpreted the biblical verse from the Song of Solomon, 'Let his left hand be under my head and his right hand embrace me', as meaning 'a married woman expressing herself with longing that her husband put his left arm under her head and that he uses his right hand to stimulate her clitoris'. As they saw it, clit rubbing was God's will, but they were also adamant that women would not be able to orgasm without submitting to their husbands.[23]

BY THE EARLY 1980S, EVEN some men's liberationists had jettisoned feminism. Warren Farrell is a case in point. By this time, he was 'the arch enemy of Shere Hite' and called her book 'The Hate Report'. While supportive of feminism in the 1970s, traces of this rightward turn can be found in his early work. By the 1980s, Farrell too offered a biological and evolutionary explanation of men's oppressive behaviour. He argued that this comes from a time 'where men competed for the most beautiful women' by killing each other off leaving women with 'the best protectors and hunters.' This 'helped survival for thousands of years'.[24] Farrell stopped believing that men oppressed women because of sexism and embraced the idea that each gender was made powerless by the other. For women, he said, the social pressure to be attractive turns them into 'sex objects', while emphasis on men having high status careers turns them into 'success objects'. But over the past twenty years feminism had 'taken a magnifying glass' to female powerlessness, neglecting the male experience of this. So now the feminist movement's focus on women's oppression had spawned 'a new sexism' against men. Farrell contended that women now had power *over men*. That men die more frequently by suicide and have shorter life expectancy than women proved this. While men were in positions of power at work, women had 'miniskirt power' and 'cleavage power'. This allowed women, even those in subordinate positions, to wield 'enormous sexual leverage over men'. He wrote, 'feminism has taught women to sue men for sexual harassment or date rape . . . no one has taught men to sue women for sexual trauma for saying "yes" then "no" then "yes" then "no."[25] According to feminist Laura Bates, Warren Farrell's turn rightward against feminism is 'representative of a much greater tear in the fabric of the men's liberation movement'.[26]

IN 1993, FARRELL PUBLISHED HIS opus, *The Myth of Male Power.* This is crucial to today's manosphere—online forums and websites littered with misogynistic, racist, conspiratorial content where men discuss sex and relationships, and YouTube and TikTok channels where men like rapist Andrew Tate and proto-fascist Jordan Peterson produce content for an audience of young men. This audience sometimes has legitimate grievances. These men are often poor, their prospects for careers and romance are limited, and they are blamed for their own failure to thrive. Other times they are middle-class men who have a zero-sum understanding of power. Any rise in the status of women and people of colour means an automatic loss for them. According to journalists Jamie Tahsin and Matt Shea, who spent time a lot of time with Andrew Tate, the manosphere is 'underpinned by a shared foundational belief that the world is being manipulated in unnatural ways' by feminists, to make life easier for women at the expense of men, who are aggrieved and victimised.[27] Though misogyny churns beneath the surface of Farrell's thinking, he is less aggressive than Tate. He is not envied in terms of his body, lifestyle, and sexual prowess the way Tate is. But his work is essential. According to sociologist Michael Kimmel, Farrell's *The Myth of Male Power* 'is the Bible' of the manosphere; 'it's really the foundational text'.[28]

Men describe the moment they realise the world is slanted in women's favour as being 'red-pilled'—the manosphere version of the feminist 'click' of consciousness raising—a reference to the moment in the *The Matrix* when Neo takes the red pill and wakes up to find machines feeding on him. To the men of the manosphere, it is feminism that keeps men docile and 'enslaved', brainwashing them to think that women are oppressed. According to journalist Mariah Blake, 'Many devotees say they had their "red pill" moment when they discovered Farrell's ideas'. This is reflected in YouTube comments; underneath an interview Farrell gave with Jordan Peterson, a user has written, 'Warren's book, *The Myth of Male Power* changed my life 20 years ago. There is no "manosphere", no "red pill" without it'. There are echoes of Farrell when Andrew Tate likens the position of women to the queen on the chess board who 'can zip across' while the king 'moves one square at a time'. Or when Tate says that for a man to own a superyacht he would have to work his whole life, but a 'girl' can just send 'one DM to a guy'.[29] Being red-pilled is an incredibly powerful moment for men, because their failure to succeed is now not their own fault, but the fault of a feminist conspiracy.

Until recently, Farrell was largely offline, but lately he has done more interviews. He appeared on the manosphere podcast *Whatever*, which has four million subscribers and episodes with clickbait titles like 'Feminist gets ROASTED' and 'Feminist Reveals Just How IRRATIONAL She Is!' In this interview, the host asked Farrell, 'Do you think that the rise of someone like Andrew Tate is the result of decades of casual misandry and the indoctrination of men and boys to view themselves as less than? [The result] of the pendulum swinging the other way?' 'Basically, yes', replied Farrell. 'All men are told is that "the future is female" and that "masculinity is toxic"'. When asked in a different interview what he thought about the violent tactics and hateful language of the manosphere, he likened these men to militant Black Power leaders such as Stokely Carmichael and Eldridge Cleaver and the misandry of feminist Valerie Solanas. He declared 'All movements need their extreme factions . . . Martin Luther King alone was dismissed'.[30]

Today's manosphere, like the backlash of the 1980s, offers men a simple explanation for their problems: They are caused by women and feminism, and only misogyny can fix them. But the feminism of the first *Hite Report* really did change sexual relations between women and men. Men's letters show how feminism touched them, took them by the hand, and sometimes led them somewhere new. It helped them to see that misogyny was no solution, as it pressures men to conform to rigid and limiting standards of masculinity and places men in hierarchical relationships with women and with each other. It makes everyone miserable. For Shere, it was about to get a lot worse.

CHAPTER 6

THE CENTRE OF THE STORM

In 1987, Ian Leslie reporting for *60 Minutes* travelled to New York to interview Shere about her book *Women and Love*, the third and final volume of the *Hite Report* trilogy, which had just been published. Leslie and his crew set up the interview in Shere's sumptuous Fifth Avenue living room. She wore her version of the eighties power suit: smart blue pinstripe trousers and blazer with a crisp white shirt. Her look was still highly feminine, with cinched waist, long flowing blond curls, red lipstick, and lacquered nails polished to a point.

Ian Leslie's opening question was: 'Why is Shere Hite so sensitive about criticism?' Shere couldn't believe it. She butted in immediately and walked across the room. She pointed her finger at Leslie, who remained seated. 'Can I finish my question?' he asked. 'No!' Shere yelled, pacing, heels clacking. 'I think you're going to keep on like this during the entire thing'. Shere pulled the camera away from her and Leslie. 'I don't care to have this part filmed. You know what you're doing', she said wagging her finger, 'you're doing exactly what the men in the book do . . . Do you want to do a decent interview?! Otherwise, go home!' She looked over his shoulder and read his notes. Outraged, she yelled: 'Now you're going to say "You've been accused of man bashing!"' As Shere towered over him, he replied calmly, still seated: 'You've been accused of man bashing . . .' She screamed: 'Yes! And it's gonna happen right here!' The shot froze on Shere looking wild, overwrought. 'And that', said Leslie calmly, 'is how we parted company with Shere Hite'.

Leslie reflected later, 'I took a terrible risk on my technique in this story. Normally when you interview a feisty subject, the first five minutes of the interview you warm them up and then you hit them with . . . the hard questions after that. I turned it round [and went] into Shere Hite with the hard questions'. So he never wanted to talk about *Women and Love* but to provoke a reaction in Shere as quickly as possible. Her emotional response was the story here, as it so often was by the late 1980s. Leslie celebrated the interview as 'one of the most entertaining I ever did'.

If only Ian Leslie was an outlier; but he wasn't even leading the hungry pack. After *Women and Love* was published, the attacks on Shere intensified. The media closed ranks, from the credible *London Review of Books* and *Washington Post* to tabloid newspapers and *Penthouse* —they all went after her. As she put it, 'The media's response was like a huge collective voice shouting "Shut up!"' As politics turned fully against feminism by the late 1980s, Shere kept speaking about how gendered power infused sex and love, that most intimate, sacred realm between men and women. If the story of the first *Hite Report* narrates the rise of feminism, its power and ability to change lives, then the trashing of

Shere Hite tells the story of the clampdown on feminism and how one woman came to stand in for an entire movement.

Shere wrote *Women and Love* to investigate a 'feeling in the early 1970s women's movement that love is an ideological construct'. Indeed, one feminist manifesto roared, 'We must destroy love. Love promotes [women's] vulnerability, dependence, possessiveness . . . and prevents full development'.[1] But Shere thought, 'We needed to analyse this concept a little more because the fact is that people do meet other people and feel very enthusiastic about individuals . . . those feelings are real and they are very enjoyable'. As we have seen, Shere also *loved* love. While working on this project, she fell in love with a man named Friedrich Höricke, a German pianist twenty years her junior. They met at a party after a classical concert at the German Consulate, and in a repeat of the way that Shere had boldly followed Martin Sage into a phone booth, she jumped into his elevator. Shere thought Höricke 'ooz[ed] beauty, sex appeal and gorgeousness'. After three months of whirlwind romance, they decided to get married. The ceremony was a grand affair, with a horse-drawn carriage to whisk the newlyweds away along with Shere's dog Rusty who sat in the front seat.

Their partnership was of great interest to the media. Shere and Höricke's performance of romance for the cameras was extraordinary. In many photos they stare into one another's eyes and kiss passionately; her apartment provides the backdrop. In some she sits astride him on his grand piano, or they kiss against her desk, which is covered in notes and Post-its. A close-up image of them leaning in for a kiss was used for the British edition of *Women and Love*. I spoke to Harriet Griffey, one of Shere's British editors, who recalled Shere saying that she loved kissing Friedrich's teeth because when the body decomposes, the teeth remain.

Shere wrote elsewhere, 'five hundred years from now when there is no more flesh, your teeth will still be there, to have been kissed by me—to know I loved you. To feel the warmth of my kiss'. Höricke tried to protect Shere when the media turned on her.

Women and Love was an ambitious book. It ran to nine hundred pages and the print was small. Shere asked four thousand women about their love lives and relationships. She had intended to include women's reflections on love in the first *Hite Report* but had run out of space. She used the same method as in the first two books. She developed a lengthy questionnaire. She asked women everything from 'Are you in love?' to 'Have you ever felt you were "owned" or suffocated, held down in a relationship . . . ?' to 'What is your favourite way to waste time?' and 'Was your mother affectionate?' As with her research on men, she mailed one hundred thousand questionnaires to women's groups across the United States, from feminist organisations to church groups and garden clubs. Then she filled the gaps to ensure a more representative sample. The statistics she generated were hugely startling: 84 percent of women were not emotionally satisfied in their relationships, 95 percent of women wished men were more emotionally open, 51 percent of divorces were filed by women. Most shocking, especially for conservatives in the United States, 70 percent of married women had affairs, about the same percentage as men, according to Shere. As British author Hilary Mantel wrote: 'These statistics do seem to contradict one's belief and everyday experience'. Indeed, they don't *feel* true. Unlike the findings of the first *Hite Report*, these statistics were not corroborated by other research, which put the rate of cheating at 15 to 20 percent for women.[2] *Women and Love* begins and ends with academic essays defending her methodology. One opens rather grandly, 'As a philosopher I believe the task of ethics or moral philosophy is to determine what the real and pressing needs of humans are . . .' Shere hoped these would act as a bulletproof vest for the book and protect it from criticism, but that didn't work.

Beyond the statistics, *Women and Love*, like the other two *Hite Reports*, contained original thinking. The book was one of the first to ask a large group of women about love and relationships since the upheavals of the women's liberation movement. Shere argued that the movement had done wonders for women's friendships. The vast majority of straight women now felt their relationship with their best friends were the most important in their lives. Lately, women's friendships have been given more attention, but long before this, testimony about friendship's power danced across the pages of *Women and Love*: 'My best-friend is like a candle that always burns. She is a constant source of energy and inspiration for me and she says I am the same for her'. Feminist friendships were often based on newfound feelings of esteem, love, and respect toward women, but sometimes, this made it difficult to express the ugly feelings that lay between friends. Feelings like envy were repressed because women felt these feelings made them bad feminists. [3] Shere gave space to 'ambivalences, interesting dynamics, difficulties and jealousies' in friendship. She calls partings of friends what they are: breakups. Women describe the pain of losing friends to romantic relationships, how difficult it is for friendship to compete with marriage and romance, which are held in such high esteem socially and always automatically prioritised: 'She got married, after which she lost her grip and decided she couldn't support two major relationships . . . The thing I miss the most [was how] I walked taller and felt invincible because I had somebody who'd fight back to back with me . . . I thought with her I had beaten the system, but I should have known the goddamn system would beat me in the end'. Others recount friendships pressurised by addiction, or bust-ups caused by political differences. One woman's friend had become an exotic dancer, and she found it 'absolutely nauseating that men just sit there and watch her'. Perhaps, because fallouts in friendships are not taken as seriously as romantic breakups, there were no cultural scripts or self-help books to guide these women, so some of them remained haunted by these endings; their ex–best friends visited them in dreams. Despite the difficulties, Shere thought women's friendships could act as a model for better, more equal relations.

Women and Love also discussed one of the biggest changes in American society. By the 1980s, the model of a nuclear family based on a male breadwinner and an unpaid housewife was largely a thing of the past; women and men now worked outside the home. While this was true much earlier for many African American couples and working-class couples, by the late 1980s it was true for most middle-class couples too.[4] In light of this upheaval, Shere asked, 'Who does the housework?' She found that care, cleaning, and what is now known as 'emotional labour' or 'social reproduction' continued to fall on women in the dual-income family. This unequal division of labour continues and has been the subject of many recent feminist books and think pieces, but Shere discussed it way back in 1987. One woman wrote: 'When I have just worked all day on four hours' sleep, am running through the rain up the driveway with six bags of groceries and the phone is ringing (and no one is answering it although both my husband and son are home) . . . what can I say?' Shere also spoke about what we now call 'coercive control', dominating behaviour in intimate relationships that is often a precursor to physical violence. This concept is usually attributed to the 2007 work of Evan Stark, though it is mentioned here long before.[5] Shere named it 'emotional harassment', and some women wrote about being routinely insulted, controlled, and punished by male partners. Shere described how this behaviour was minimised: 'The perpetrator will need never answer, will never be called to justice'. Today coercive control is taken more seriously, so this is not always the case.

The book recounted story after story of women's unhappiness in their relationships with men. Shere asked, 'Should women take a mass vacation from trying to understand men?' She gave space to women who proposed collective solutions, including a 'national strike, a boycott, a new version of *Lysistrata*', a reference to Aristophanes' classical Greek play in which the women go on sex strike. But despite women's misery, Shere remained optimistic. The high rate of adultery and divorce instigated by women was already a kind of strike, evidence of individual rebellion against a system causing them pain. Their widespread despair marked not malaise but 'a midpoint in the feminist revolution'. Shere, who revelled in the poetic, put it like this: 'Women are "astronauts" gazing at the whole system of male ideology from orbit', they were questioning their lives. This would lead to 'a new world still in process of formation . . . a star, twinkling with light and motion'.

Unlike the first *Hite Report*, which opened up possibilities for sex beyond rigid gender roles, *Women and Love* was essentialist. This book celebrated women's capacity to care and nurture against men's rationality and emotional silence, a strand of thought prevalent in feminism in the 1980s.[6] It did not see men and women's behaviours as the result of sexist conditioning but toyed with the idea that women were innately more nurturing. Gender was still the only lens Shere used to analyse women, though by now feminism was broadening its scope and developing an 'intersectional' viewpoint. While Kimberlé Crenshaw coined this term two years after *Women and Love* was published, the idea was rooted in histories of Black and Third World feminist theory.[7] Intersectionality described how women's experience of gender and gender oppression was always modulated by other elements of identity such as race and class. It also made clear that the implicit subject of feminism was a white woman, the movement based on her norms and needs and then extended out to other women. Shere did not integrate these insights into *Women and Love*. She wrote that 'the focus of this study is on not class', or indeed race, 'but the experiences women have in common because of their gender'. She maintained that in relationships 'variables such as class . . . [and] race are not nearly as influential as the overall experience of being female'. But this doesn't seem true when reading the testimony of women of colour in *Women and Love*. One woman wrote: 'I'm a twenty-five-year-old black woman . . . I am trying to get a career, but at this point in time it looks so far away. My biggest problem right now is having to depend on a man to survive. There are no jobs here. Unemployment in Detroit is 25 percent. [My boyfriend and I] fight about money most frequently. Nobody wins'. Her experience is gendered certainly, but it is impossible to say that gender here is the *most* influential element in her story, considering that her experience of gender cannot be separated from her sexuality, from being Black, or from being working class.

There were other limits to the book too. Shere didn't consider how the rise of the dual-income couple and family was due to deindustrialisation and neoliberalism as well as women's liberation. Shere suggested that 'women here say they work because they like to have a life of their own' and don't want to be financially dependent on a partner. That's true, but it was also the case that by the late 1980s, two incomes were required to keep a couple or a family afloat. Shere scare-quoted this as an 'explanation', suggesting it 'suited the needs of an ideology that doesn't want to believe women are changing'. But the woman's testimony above shows something different. She was willing to change, and because of the women's liberation movement she hoped for a career, but there were no jobs in rapidly deindustrialising Detroit. The year *Women and Love* came out, the Detroit Cadillac plant laid off three thousand workers.[8]

The media didn't care for nuance. They were disinterested in the argument of the book and the intimate testimonies that offered a glimpse into women's lives. They didn't engage her in vigorous debate about the book's possibilities and limits. Instead, they intensified the critiques they made about the first two books. They focused on her 'fake stats' and 'false methods'.'Shere Hite and the trouble with numbers', said *The Washington Post*. 'Only unhappy women are likely to take the time to answer 127 essay questions, and thus her sample is representative only of the discontented'. Perhaps the critics had a point. Some of the questions seem designed to capture discontent; consider: 'Are you jealous? Of friendships? Other Women? Men?' Who could truthfully have written 'no, never' to that? Shere defended her methodology. In *Woman and Love* she made it clear that the stats reflected only women who had answered, not the entire population, but this was ambiguous in the book's promotion.

Time magazine called Shere to tell her she would be their cover story. She was excited, but the headline screamed: 'Are Women Fed Up?: A hotly disputed *Hite Report* says yes—and that men are to blame'. The image showed a woman yelling at a man, who looks the epitome of henpecked. The review read: 'Hite's analysis is colored by her entrenched view that most men are treacherous troglodytes and women are socially conditioned to serve them. The survey often seems merely to provide for the author's own male-bashing diatribes'.We see why Shere was attacked: She was a feminist. It wasn't just her but that the women who filled out the questionnaire were all feminists too. The book has nothing to say about the majority of American women, because it is only 'full of extreme views of strident women' who are 'malcontents'. Then she went on *Oprah* and was scapegoated for the entire women's movement. She faced an all-male audience. Men queued at the microphone to accuse her: 'What I'm complaining about is the approach which began with women's lib. Since then men have been murdered and [women] have gotten away with it. We've had our children taken away, we've had our homes taken away, we've had our jobs taken away'. These men blamed her, a proxy for feminism, for any suffering any woman had ever caused them.

DESPITE CONDEMNING SHERE'S WORK FOR its feminist bias, the media often used biased studies to push their own conservative agenda, not bothering to interrogate the methodology or ideological underpinnings. One of the most cited at this time was a study done by Harvard and Yale in 1986 that found that college-educated women aged forty had a less than 2 percent chance of marrying. This was incorrect but was widely quoted and cemented the idea of the desperate single woman.[9] *Newsweek* screamed, 'Women over 40 more likely to be killed by a terrorist than get married'. This study so pierced the zeitgeist that it became a plot point in Nora Ephron's film *Sleepless in Seattle*. Meg Ryan wailed that while the statistic might not be true, 'it feels true'. This is the anti-feminist mirror to the iconic moment in Ephron's earlier film *When Harry Met Sally*, where Meg Ryan fakes an orgasm over a pastrami sandwich. When the study was found to be false, hardly any journalists bothered to correct themselves. Filmmaker Ann Eugenia Volks wrote a letter in support of Shere. She compared the media's response to *Women and Love* to its treatment of the Harvard/Yale study, concluding, 'Clearly this is not about methodology but the message'.

Shere was subjected to increasingly personal attacks. The *Chicago Tribune* called '*Women and Love* a hopeless mess of shoddy thinking, questionable methodology, knee-jerk sociology and infantile philosophy . . . [a] monument to dim-wittedness. How many Shere Hite's does it take to change a lightbulb? There cannot be enough'. Shere found this hard to take, and acted out. The media lapped it up, denied their role in her downfall, and called her crazy. In November, *Newsweek* ran an article about the 'bizarre month for sex researcher Shere Hite'. They described her posing as her own secretary, a woman named Diana Gregory who called journalists to berate them for their treatment of Shere. Shere told *The Washington Post* that Gregory had worked for her for four years. *The Post* tried to track down 'the elusive Diana'. They called Shere's publisher, Knopf, and were told, 'No one has ever met or seen or spoken with Diana Gregory'. *The Post* asked Shere why she didn't thank Diana Gregory in the acknowledgments of *Women and Love*. She forgot, she explained. Reporters then found out that Shere's middle names were Diana and Gregory. There was uproar. She maintained this was just a coincidence, and so was the fact that their voices were similar: 'In the Midwest, a lot of people sound the same'. The press was not convinced. They visited Shere at her Fifth Avenue apartment. She introduced them to a woman pretending to be Diana. The journalists asked this woman for identification. 'What is this, a witch hunt?' asked Shere. Höricke asked the press to leave. *The Post* employed a handwriting expert to compare Shere's penmanship with Diana Gregory's. He concluded, of course, that the handwriting was the same. *Newsweek* declared Shere 'a pop-culture demagogue, caught in the glare of public scrutiny and frantically dithering away whatever credibility she may once have had'.

The press went wild after she struck a limo driver, Frank Nicoletti. He came to pick her up for an appearance on the talk show *Sally Jessy Raphael*. She kept him waiting for almost an hour while he repeatedly rang the buzzer and Shere assured him that she'd be down soon. Eventually she did appear, but Nicoletti had to relay the news that there was no way they could get to the studio on time and she 'freaked out'. Shere could fly off the handle and behave unreasonably if she felt someone had slighted her. Often low-paid workers bore the brunt. She would turn against waitstaff or scream at taxi drivers, publicists, and staff on the lower rungs at publishing houses who sometimes refused to work with her. When having coffee with the British journalist Polly Toynbee in her dressing room, she 'sent someone to fetch her a coffee cup from a distant room because it was so much prettier than an almost identical cup in front of her'. But those who were close to her also suffered; as her ex-boyfriend Martin Sage remarked, 'She was an equal opportunity insulter'.

The media found her hijinks irresistible. The *New York Post* ran the headline 'Shere Hite Slugs Limousine Driver', and asked whether 'Shere Hite's next project will be an exhaustively researched book on female violence'. Two days later she was interviewed by Maury Povich on *A Current Affair*. Povich set a trap and invited a surprise guest, Frank Nicoletti. She yanked off her earpiece, pushed the camera away, and stalked out, yelling that Povich was 'acting like the men in her book' and had 'lied to get this interview'. She went back on *The Phil Donahue Show* because Donahue gave the first *Hite Report* such a positive hearing, but the reception could not have been more different. One woman later wrote to Shere, expressing her dismay: 'I just knew that of all the men to give you a fair shake, it would be Phil. Was I wrong . . .' He wouldn't discuss the book, focussing only on the limo driver and the intrigue with Diana Gregory. The audience jeered. At the time, this reporting was celebrated as sound investigative journalism. As *Newsweek* put it, this was just the 'glare of public scrutiny', but looking back, it seems harassing. Rather than report or offer analysis, the aim was to pull Shere down.

There was no curiosity about why Shere would act this way. She seems to me a woman under immense pressure, whose book does have some methodological flaws, but who was never given a fair hearing because of its political content. She made up secretarial staff to defend herself to journalists because she wished she had that kind of support. She found rejection immensely difficult. If she felt her contribution was insufficiently garlanded, she was prone to overreact.

Shere was genuinely perplexed about why the media monstered her. After all, the methodology and conclusions of *Women and Love* were not so different from the first or second *Hite Report*. Sexism got right between the sheets and hid under the bed, as she said in the first book; it stifled men's lives as well as women's, as she showed in the second. In the third, she told how it lurked in the dishwater and on the dinner date. Women still needed feminism, which didn't seem so revolutionary to her. She was confused: 'It was like walking through a dark, unfamiliar room, bumping into things. You turn on the light but none of them work. You can't get any of them to work . . . I'm not sure we ever got to the bottom of what was going on, as the bigger dimensions were hard to see'. We can flick the light on, though, and illuminate the political context for the attacks. We can see what happened to Shere.

BY 1987, REAGAN HAD BEEN in office for seven years, pushing anti-feminism. He described his agenda as 'family values', a way to reassert patriarchal authority while seeming neutral, as the historian Kristin Kobes Du Mez explains.[10] The family Reagan conjured was a white conservative Christian family. He combined 'family values' with the economics of neoliberalism, he made sweeping welfare cuts, and he defanged wealth redistribution from the rich to the poor by lowering taxes. Reagan's cuts meant what they always do—women picked up the slack in families and took care of children and elders, and poor and often racialised women fell, along with their families, into greater poverty.[11] To get his cuts through, Reagan created the racist bogeywoman, the 'welfare queen' who is almost always an African American mother allegedly living in luxury through committing welfare fraud. In times of backlash, women who do feminist work, like Shere, are individually targeted, but so are entire groups of women who are often the most vulnerable in society.

During the early years of his presidency, Reagan saw communism as the biggest threat to U.S. society. But by 1987, feminism had replaced communism as one of *the* premier existential threats facing the United States. It seemed like the States would be triumphant: This was the year when Reagan would travel to Berlin and implore Mikhail Gorbachev to 'Tear down this wall'. Glasnost (*transparency*) and perestroika (*restructuring*) were already remaking the USSR. It is often presumed that the end of the Cold War was a triumphant moment for those on the right of politics. In fact, historian Quinn Slobodian has shown, as McDonald's opened in Moscow, the mood was decidedly morbid. The Cold War may have been won against communism, but, as American conservatives saw it, 'Leviathan lived on'. The enemy had simply shape-shifted from the red half of the world into the movement for feminism, environmentalism, and civil rights. These social movements had injected poison into the body politic'. By the 1980s, people had grown dependent on the government, they were 'addicted' to using public money to right social inequalities. [12]

The political work of right-wing women like Phyllis Schlafly, Anita Bryant, and Beverley LaHaye meant by 1987 feminists were no longer seen to represent the majority and no longer had the credibility to speak on behalf of all women. Right-wing women claimed that feminists were a small, bedraggled minority who were not representative but used devious means to get power and infiltrate the government, and to hold the majority of women—happy homemakers—hostage. LaHaye founded conservative women's organisation Concerned Women for America after seeing Betty Friedan claim NOW represented *all* American women. As CWA grew rapidly, LaHaye announced, 'No longer do feminists have a monopoly. No longer can they claim to speak for *all* American women. We are here, hundreds of thousands now, telling the world that feminism is a false view'.[13] Right-wing women saw themselves as 'a little flock pitted against a formidable array of [feminist] forces—the President, the federal bureaucracy, the mushrooming feminist organizations . . . Yet we believed the Lord's admonition: "Know ye truth, and the truth (not Women's Lib) shall make you free." (John 8:32)'.[14]

Initially, feminists maintained that right-wing women were a lunatic fringe, underestimating their reach and organising power. Gloria Steinem declined to debate Phyllis Schlafly, as she didn't want her minority opinion to be given more airtime. Other feminists debated her, but this often did the cause more harm than good. Betty Friedan lost control, saying to Schlafly, 'I'd like to burn you at the stake'.[15] Marc Feigen Fasteau, who we met in the last chapter and his wife, lawyer Brenda Feigen Fasteau, debated Schlafly and her husband. To bolster one of her points, Phyllis made up a legal case, which Brenda asked her to state. This left Schlafly open-mouthed, unable to name that case because it didn't exist.[16] Yet I wondered as I read Brenda Feigen's memoir how many viewers would have seen this as humiliation of an 'ordinary' housewife by an 'elite' feminist lawyer, showing feminists to be an out-of-touch minority. It was Andrea Dworkin who first asked why right-wing women cut through with so many. Dworkin theorised that right-wing women addressed the fear of male violence, a concern held by the vast majority of women. Right-wing women promised safety through submission. They displaced male violence onto the stranger, the migrant, the Black man, the man waiting in the dark alley. The need to be protected from this violence 'intensified the loyalty of women to men'—to husbands and fathers—who certainly are dangerous but are 'at least known quantities'.[17] The idea that feminists no longer represented the interests of all women was behind the attacks on Shere. The media discredited her by saying that she, and the women she surveyed, were a disgruntled minority, which did not reflect how the majority of women felt. Women's letters to Shere at this time also reflect this change; women praise *Women and Love* but see the movement's members as outliers, writing, 'I'm not a bra-burning feminist'.

Right-wing women also argued that feminism made women miserable. Feminism attempted to liberate women from what was most fulfilling to them. Phyllis Schlafly wrote, 'The principal purpose of [this] shrill tirade is to sow seeds of discontent among happy, married women'.[18] Feminism said that 'women can have it all', but right-wing women said the ashen faces of stressed and tired working mothers told another story. As Susan Faludi wrote, the idea that feminism made women unhappy seeped into the culture and was key to the backlash. The film *Fatal Attraction*, one of the most misogynistic films ever made, was the epitome of this. It came out the same year as *Women and Love*, and many readers saw it. *Fatal Attraction* blamed feminism for women's unhappiness. In this film, Glenn Close plays an unmarried career woman. She is jilted by her lover and embarks on a reign of terror: stalking, kidnapping, boiling beloved pet rabbits on the stove until she is killed off by the stay-at-home mom. One Fox executive described it as 'the psychotic manifestation of the *Newsweek* marriage study'. Michael Douglas, the leading man, thought the film was great because he was 'sick of feminists with their unreasonable demands'.[19] Shere mused on *Fatal Attraction*: 'It could be asked whether this film is an indication of the returning power of the medieval church doctrines about women'. She saw what she endured reflected in the film's treatment of the single woman: 'Women must be married and have children to be accepted into society, women who focus mostly on their careers, are sexual, must be punished'.

Many readers wrote to Shere to tell her that along with her book, they were reading *Women Who Love Too Much* by Robin Norwood. This book came out in 1985 and was on the *New York Times* bestseller list for much of 1987. It doesn't blame feminism for women's unhappiness, it blames women. It explored the common pattern of women's destructive, unhappy relationships with men. Norwood framed this as an addiction, describing women as 'man junkies' because of patterns rooted in childhood. There is no doubt that many women found the book a profound relief. One woman wrote to Shere, 'I gave up a 5 year career because I was emotionally dead and physically exhausted from my 20 year marriage. I read *Women Who Love Too Much*, went into therapy for the last year and a half and now your book is getting me the rest of the way'.

Shere discussed Norwood's book in *Women and Love*; it wasn't that 'women loved too much' but that the world needed to change. Norwood focussed wholly on the individual. As Faludi remarked, Norwood does not 'ever turn the tables: her book asks why so many women "choose" abusive men, but not why there are so many abusive men to choose from'.[20] Nor did Norwood discuss how cuts to welfare, housing, and women's shelters under Reagan made it harder for women to leave. Or how in a sexist society there will always be 'women who love too much'. Instead, Norwood helped women to cope, to change themselves rather than the world. In this way she resembled the psychoanalysis women accessed in a time before women's liberation, as I discussed in chapter two. Shere hoped that questioning their relationships would lead women to then challenge the entire social structure, but this was not guaranteed. By 1987, the tools for liberation had changed and become individualised. Many women stopped with themselves. The personal had become personal again, shorn of its politics.

The vilification of Shere went on and on, 'one never knew when or from what quarter, for many gruelling months'. Fox TV, which would soon become Fox News, got in on the game. This network set up operations in 1986 and began attacks on Shere in 1987. In a move presaging the relentless, aggressive, twenty-four-hour reporting they would become famous for, they stationed a reporter outside Shere's apartment. They intended to hound her until she behaved badly, then present this 'as the "awful truth" about me', she wrote. Fox's reporting broadcast Shere's address, and she began to receive threatening messages from reporters on her answering machine and death threats in the post.

Shere was targeted because she was famous. That is why she was the scapegoat for feminism, rather than someone like Andrea Dworkin. She also didn't have a handle on the press like that other gorgeous, famous feminist, Gloria Steinem. Unlike Steinem, who is known for her poise, when Shere behaved badly, she screamed, yelled, ran out of the studio jewellery jangling; it was such a spectacularly *visual* performance, so perfect for television. This reaction could be provoked almost on cue and then filmed, which was great for a network's bottom lines. As Monica Lewinsky said of her own very public shaming ten years after Shere's, 'The more shame, the more clicks, the more clicks, the more advertising dollars'.[21] Feminists including Steinem, Kate Millett, Ntozake Shange, and Barbara Ehrenreich did eventually come to Shere's defence, signing a statement and presenting it at the American Studies Association conference. They wrote that 'important issues that concern women's lives are being obscured and trivialised by the media's assault on Shere Hite . . . The attack on Hite's work is part of the the current conservative backlash. These attacks are not so much directed against a single woman as they are directed against the rights of women everywhere'. This was an important statement, but hardly touched by the media.

This campaign took a huge emotional and financial toll on Shere. She borrowed money against her mortgage to finance the research for *Women and Love*, intending to pay it back when the paperback rights were sold in the States, but no one bought them. 'I had to sell the apartment. I have not had such a beautiful home since'. She and Höricke packed up the Fifth Avenue apartment into boxes and fled to Europe. She turned herself in at the German embassy—Höricke's country of origin—reneging her U.S. passport, identifying dramatically as 'a political refugee'. She and Höricke eventually split, and Shere moved peripatetically between Paris and London, not settling again until the very last years of her life. In her memoir, she wrote, 'I have never lived in one place for very long . . . mostly staying in hotels! I love hotels because in a hotel, someone else takes care of you', but life without a fixed address wasn't that easy.

In London, Shere began a relationship with journalist and writer Joanna Briscoe, who, like her ex-husband, was twenty years her junior. When we spoke, Briscoe told me they first met when she interviewed Shere. Briscoe thought, 'This is odd, she's flirting with me', odd because it was an interview and she had presumed Shere was straight, 'but she was definitely flirting'. She described Shere as 'charming beyond charming . . . A newspaper delivered her flowers and she gave them to me and I just floated out of there'. Shere lived between Briscoe's Bloomsbury apartment—'which was very exciting. Here was my heroine and crush in my flat!'—and a squatted council house where she stayed on a small mattress on the floor. But she also engaged in celebrity behaviour; she would skip off to Paris and 'stay in the Hilton, when it was posher than it is now', or fly to Hamburg to get her hair cut, take a taxi and keep the meter running all day, or spend thousands on clothes. Shere had all her post directed to the Paris Hilton and would charm the concierges into running errands for her whether she was staying there or not. Briscoe witnessed Shere passing her handbag over and asking the staff if they could get it mended for her. People often really wanted to please her: 'They would do anything for her. She was so charismatic, so well dressed, and when she wanted to be, she could be really charming'.

There were some wonderful times between Briscoe and Shere. Briscoe stressed that 'she was amazing. Really not like other people'. They would go out to dinner together. Shere would order steaks, then wrap up the leftovers and put them in her handbag. They would go shopping. Shere introduced Briscoe to vintage clothing before it was a thing. Or they would watch old movies from the 1940s on Briscoe's couch and have long, interesting discussions about politics and feminism. But Shere was not easy. As we have seen, she was highly sensitive and thin-skinned. This made her a difficult houseguest, liable to fly off the handle at a perceived slight or injustice, yell and scream, then withdraw for days under the guise that 'she was resting her voice', communicating only via handwritten note. She would sometimes lecture Briscoe's friends about feminism or disengage from a conversation if it didn't centre her. 'I cannot exaggerate, it really had to be all about her', Briscoe said. Shere rightly thought her own contribution was huge and was feeling the neglect of the press, of feminists, and of society. Sometimes, though, she'd overstate the case. She asked a friend of Briscoe's 'whether it had occurred to you that I have replaced Freud . . . It was a mix between grandiosity and sadness'.

Shere refused to accept that the press had abandoned her. She sent endless faxes to journalists offering interviews and articles 'to keep my writing afloat'. There are hundreds of these sent from the Paris Hilton. Shere's desperation comes through in the archive. A woman wrote to her telling her how much she loved *The Hite Report* and asking whether Shere might publish a concise edition. Shere made a note on the letter: 'if she's in New York call her!' as if this stranger might be able to get this next venture off the ground and put her back in the spotlight. She could be quite an instrumentalist, or, as Briscoe put it, 'pretty takey'. She often noted on her letters what people might be able to do for her, like 'ask her for a column'. She kept working, of course, through the night like she always did. She did publish further books, including *The Hite Report on the Family* and *Good Guys, Bad Guys and Other Lovers*, along with reassessments of *The Hite Report*. While these were quite well received, they weren't published in the States, and nothing was ever as big as the first book. There was no equivalent astronomical rise, and the attention was never enough. Sometimes, when Shere stayed with her, Briscoe wasn't sure how much work was actually going on and how much she was just moving her hundreds of Post-its and napkins around in the dark.

IN 1991, SHERE WATCHED FROM London as African American law professor Anita Hill testified against the first Black Supreme Court nominee, Clarence Thomas. Hill had been sexually harassed by Thomas, her former boss in the public service. This came to light when he had been nominated to the Supreme Court. She was called to testify and was asked to recount Thomas's treatment of her, how he insisted on telling her about pornography he'd enjoyed and his own sexual prowess. An all-white, all-male panel of senators interrogated her. They asked: Are you a scorned woman? Is this a fantasy? Do you want to be famous? Thomas likened his treatment to a 'high-tech lynching' and was appointed as a Supreme Court justice. Hill was disgraced and shamed. Journalist David Brock published the hit job *The Real Anita Hill*, in which he tried to dredge up anything 'a little bit nutty and a little bit slutty' about her. All kinds of media presumed this book was true, and it spent 14 weeks on the *New York Times* bestseller list. [22]

Watching Anita Hill was an important moment for Shere. 'I suddenly saw clearly the "why" of the very personal attack on me . . . that what was happening to her, and what happened to me . . . was a type of rape trial scenario . . . a sort of public rape in newsprint'. Shere's identification with Hill may not be immediately obvious; certainly there are differences between them. Hill is Black and Shere was white, Hill was sexually harassed before her trial, and in Shere's case there was no such original event, no rape before the rape trial. Regardless of the differences, it is true that the treatment of women at the rape trial leaks out into the treatment women get when they talk publicly about the way sex is infused with power. Anita Hill made Shere realise that 'any woman who talks about "sex" deserves what she gets'.

As Shere wrote, both were told, in different ways, 'she's making it up!' As if they had lots to gain by falsely accusing men of sexual harassment or talking about how sex is sexist out loud, in public. This is because, as historian Joanna Bourke shows, historically rape accusations were seen as an easy way for poor women to blackmail men into marriage. Women who made accusations of rape were thought to be in it for the money. These old ideas of women as 'hysterical, psychopathic, notoriety-seeking, or simply vicious' cling to those who make accusations in the present.[23] But women don't gain power or money from rape accusations, which are most often costly, economically and reputationally. Shere initially got rich from *The Hite Report* but then she was scorned, was shown to be a fool, suffered financially, and was forced to leave the States. The way the press invaded her privacy also resembled the rape trial. The press picked over everything, 'from my clothes, to my hair, to my apartment, to my habits and my friends', she wrote. Shere felt this echoed the way that sexual history is used in the rape trial, the way women's sexual experiences and choice of clothing are used to determine whether they 'asked for it', whether they can be believed or not. In Shere's case, the fact that she wrote so publicly about sex and had worked in porn gave the press free rein to pick over her private life, to find out if she, like the woman who wore the short skirt, had brought it on herself.

This is why you might not have heard of *The Hite Report* or Shere Hite before reading this book. Despite being one of the bestselling books of all time and bringing the insight that sex was sexist to men, to women, to the suburbs, and around the world, these attacks did their job to slander Shere and her work. She really disappeared, was disappeared; the culture opened its jaws and swallowed her up. Her ideas swirl all around us, but largely they are not attributed to their singular, strange, visionary creator, who clung on for dear life but eventually fell, or really was pushed, out of the frame.

EPILOGUE

On my final day in the archive, I found a Polaroid of Shere, taken in Paris in the late 1990s. She is turned away from the camera, sitting at a desk, in a silk slip dress, nude stockings, and suspenders. She is working, of course. She is thin and willowy, and dwarfed by the mess. All around her is chaos: Bags and jewels are strewn across the floor, a rose is haphazardly placed in a vase, and everywhere there are papers, endless papers, in messy piles, on every surface. The walls are lined with photos of her in her glory days.

Looking at this Polaroid one way, it seems the saddest in the archive. It also appeared to be a prophesy of her difficult ending. In 2020, Shere died of corticobasal degeneration, a rare neurological disorder. She was in the company of her partner, Paul Sullivan, who she lived with in London. By the end she was really unwell and couldn't speak—a real tragedy, as Regina Ryan said, 'given all the ideas she had'. Death comes for all of us, and it's often messy and undignified.

Looking at the photo a different way, she seems as resolute as ever to sit up tall and get on with her work no matter what they say about her, no matter the mess she is in. I imagined her turning toward me and saying, steely, determined, and advocating for her own relevance as always: 'You need me'. And I think we do; we need Shere Hite and *The Hite Report*. We need her because while you might not have heard of her and her work before reading this book, the right-wing attacks on her and the backlash she lived through likely have a recognisable ring to them. She showed that if you hold a mirror up to sex, you see women's place in society reflected back. But perhaps Shere's time also holds up a mirror to our own—not a perfect reflection, maybe a little fun house, but the resemblances are definitely there.

Then, as now, the right draws on biological explanations of gender difference to establish, defend, and celebrate oppressive gender roles. The fall of Roe and statewide bans that criminalise abortion even in cases of rape and incest give a clear message that cisgender women's biological capacity to bear children should be borne out in their social role as mothers, and that women should always put themselves last. In right-wing grassroots online communities both tradwives and manosphere influencers offer pseudobiological explanations for men and women's different social positions. They suggest that we all should give up on equality and revert to our 'natural' traditional roles, where *he* works outside the home and *she* is the 'queen of the household'.[1]

As in the 1980s, the right also celebrates a particular kind of family, which they imagine as biological, heterosexual, nuclear, and white. U.S. vice president JD Vance recently expressed admiration for Hungary's right-wing prime minister, Viktor Orbán, who offered loans to couples who marry, and to amnesty that loan if they have three or more children. Vance asked, 'Why can't we do that here? Why can't we actually promote family formation?' His voting record makes it clear he has a specific kind of family in mind, as he is against invitro fertilisation and gay marriage, which are both family-forming tools. [2] In his imagined family, women will be doing all the work of raising children at home, since he is against state-subsidized daycare.

Today, the right fortifies the nation as bordered, ordered, and racially homogenous through attacking migrants and racialised people. As Andrea Dworkin wrote of right-wing women in the 1980s, so today the right dislodges violence against women most often perpetrated within the family onto the stranger, the racialised man, the Muslim, the migrant, who allegedly bring rape into the West from foreign countries. In the summer of 2025, far-right riots gripped Britain. The reason given by rioters was ostensibly the rape of women and girls by migrant men. But they are rapists against rape. Many men in the far-right have convictions for domestic violence and sexual assault themselves. They see white women as the property of white men and the rape of white women by racialised men as an attack on their own unimpeded sexual access and power. It is this logic that lies under Trump's declaration that 'I want to protect the women of our country . . . whether the women like it or not, I'm gonna protect them from migrants coming in'.[3]

Currently, male violence against women is also dislodged onto trans women. They are painted as a threat, interlopers who invade women's spaces and prey on women there, rather than as subjected to male violence, as cisgendered women are. As with gay men and lesbians from the mid-1970s, the right paints trans people as paedophiles, or as disrupting the sanctity of the nuclear family by recruiting children and turning them trans or queer.[4] Anita Bryant's campaign against gay rights rested on the idea that gay men were abusers, but the right also extended this to lesbians. Dworkin interviewed right-wing women at the 1977 National Women's Conference, Houston. She found they 'consistently spoke to me about lesbians as if lesbians were rapists, certified committers of sexual assault against women and girls'. Then as now, 'no facts can intrude on this psychosexual fantasy'.[5] There has also been a widespread panic over toilets. In some U.S. states, it is now illegal for trans people to use any other bathroom than the one corresponding to the sex they were assigned at birth. The right's focus on toilets is not new; campaigning against the Equal Rights Amendment, right-wing women claimed the ERA would forcibly integrate men and women's bathrooms. Echoing today's pronoun panic, right-wing women indulged in anti-ERA street theatre, dressing up as toilets labelled 'theirs'.[6]

The manosphere vehemently accuses feminism of conspiring against men and making their lives miserable, and a growing choir of voices decries its effect on women. In this way, tradwives echo the backlash of the 1980s. They suggest that feminism makes women unhappy by making women 'think we can work 40+ hours a week, raise kids, keep a beautiful home and have time for our husbands. We can't'. To tradwives today, as to right-wing women of this earlier period, feminism is a conspiracy backed by powerful elites. Tradwives argue that feminism 'programmes' women and *forces* them to work, robbing them of the 'joy of children and motherhood'. Today's conspiratorial thinking sometimes has an anti-capitalist edge. As one tradwife influencer put it: 'Feminism is a lie corporations created to get more workers and more money'.[7] The growth of the New Right in the mid-1970s was partly a response to how economic crises combined with feminism were felt in families and workplaces. Today's tradwives are partly a response to economic conditions that have deteriorated since the 2008 financial crisis and the Covid-19 pandemic. They speak to women's real dissatisfaction with 'lean in' and 'boss babe' hustle feminism, combined with the ongoing expectation that women do all the reproductive labour at home. But the solutions they pose are wrong;

they blame it on feminism, not neoliberal capitalism, and they give up their autonomy for a 1950s cottage-core candy-land fantasy.[8]

The backlash against Shere took place under Reagan. According to the historian Gil Troy, he was the first U.S. president who was able to create an atmosphere 'conveying complex ideas in short, friendly sound-bites that stirred the American soul'. Trump is also master of pulling a mood rabbit out of a MAGA hat; Troy notes how he similarly 'improvis[es] a narrative about the present and the future rooted in American's mythic past'.[9] More than in Shere's time, today's right is a global, internationally coordinated phenomenon, with authoritarian populism on the rise everywhere and leaders in power from India to Italy, the United States to Argentina. Shere helps us to understand that our movement against the right must be global. She can teach us something too: Her *Hite Report* reached millions of people. Through sheer grit and determination, she took feminism well beyond the the usual suspects to reach people who had never heard such ideas before, and won over many who disagreed. At the moment, the right is much better at this than the left. We might also learn from Shere's mistakes and take the grassroots activism of those beyond the Global North, of those who are pushing back against the right seriously, from Warsaw to Rio, Mumbai to Gaza. We might learn from their tactics and their political thought.

Ultimately, we need Shere for her vision of sexual liberation. She changed sex forever and taught us about the importance of female pleasure. She reassured millions that they were not abnormal, though society's ideas of sex certainly were. *The Hite Report* was a bombshell, a breath of fresh air, and because of her, thousands of women had their 'click' moment. Shere explained that sex could mean something different from the usual routine of foreplay, penetration, and intercourse, ending in male orgasm. Sex could be more varied, less rigid, more equal, less exploitative, less same-old-same-old. Women could start by speaking up; they could go after pleasure and do it themselves during sex. But for sex to become its most satisfying required fulsome feminist change. Liberation meant desires would develop differently, would transform the bedroom from a space of subordination for so many, especially so many women, into a site of liberation. Shere didn't live to see that fulsome change. It is my wild wish, my passionate desire, that we still might.

ACKNOWLEDGMENTS

Many thanks to Michelle Capone, my fantastic editor, who improved this book so much. Thanks to my wonderful agent, Kate Johnson, who is a great champion of this project and my work.

Thanks to the wonderful librarians and archivists at the Schlesinger Library on the History of Women in America at Harvard University. This book would not have been possible without you. Thanks to the Institute of Advanced Studies in the Humanities at the University of Edinburgh, the Schlesinger Library, King's College London, and the Leverhulme Trust for their research fellowships.

Thanks to all of those who told me about their lives with Shere: Joanna Briscoe, Martin Sage, Regina Ryan, Mike Wilson, Dylan Landis, and Harriet Griffey.

Thanks to all my brilliant friends and my entire family. Very special thanks to my parents, Katharine Symonds and Tim Campbell. Nell Campbell, it is such fun to be your sister—thank you.

I am grateful to those who read chapters and talked through the ideas with me. Thank you to James Angel, Andrea D'Cruz, Alice Robson, Hil Aked, Taushif Kara, Laura Schwartz, Laura Doan, Alecia Simmonds, Clare Fisher, Emma Gattey, Charlotte Oakes, Julia Laite, Hannah Yoken, Victor Strazzeri, Paula Keller, Roseanna Webster, Anna Nasser, Erin Geraghty, Elly Robson Dezateux, Kath Kenny, and James Keating; the work is better for you all, and I am grateful.

Special thanks to Lucy Delap. I learn so much from you.

Thank you to Paul Morrow, Claire Shepherd, and Tanja Zeljic, who supported me juggling writing and teaching from the beginning.

Thank you to Leila Prasad, Clare Quinn, and Chandra Quinn Prasad, who regularly make my day.

I am grateful to everyone I have done politics with over the years, especially feminists and those in the London Renters Union. I remain committed to 'a sharing of life's glories', as the old tune goes. I will return to meetings soon.

Thank you to Joe Ball for transnational friendship and your belief in me. Thank you to Sass Hunt for never doubting I could write a book.

And to Ali Mussell, who read every word and who makes it possible. I love you so much.

ENDNOTES

NOTES TO PROLOGUE

1 ‘The 30 Best Selling Books of All Time’, *Newsweek*, September 30, 2021.

2 Kate Van Syckle, ‘The Man Who’s Putting More Sex Toys on Walmart’s Shelves’, *New York Times*, July 3 2019,

3 Elizabeth A. Mahar, Laurie B. Mintz, and Bianna M.Akers, ‘Orgasm Equality: Scientific Findings and Societal Implications’, *Current Sexual Health Reports* 12 (2020): 24–32.

4 For example: Sandra M. Gilbert and Susan Gubar, *Still Mad: American Writers and the Feminist Imagination* (W.W. Norton, 2021); Alice Echols, *Daring to be Bad: Radical Feminism in America 1967–1975* (University of Minnesota Press, 1989); Rachel Blau DuPlessis and Ann Snitow, *The Feminist Memoir Project: Voices from Women’s Liberation* (Three Rivers Press, 1998); Clara Bingham, *The Movement: How Women’s Liberation Transformed America* (Simon & Schuster, 2024); it is mentioned in passing in Ruth Rosen, *The World Split Open: How the Modern Women’s Movement Changed America* (Viking, 2000), 157. Even in books dedicated to feminist bestsellers or sex and women’s

liberation, *The Hite Report* doesn't feature: Imelda Whelehan, *The Feminist Bestseller: From Sex and the Single Girl to Sex and the City* (Palgrave Macmillan, 2005); Anthea Taylor, *Celebrity and the Feminist Blockbuster* (Palgrave Macmillan, 2016); Jane F. Gerhard, *Desiring Revolution: Second-Wave Feminism and the Rewriting of American Sexual Thought 1920–1982* (Columbia University Press, 2001).

5 Blanche Wiesen Cook quoted in Clare Hemmings, *Considering Emma Goldman: Feminist Political Ambivalence and the Imaginative Archive* (Duke University Press, 2018), 21.

6 The United States, for example: bell hooks, *Ain't I A Woman: Black Women and Feminism* (Pluto Press, 1982); the collected essays in Gloria T. Hull, Patricia Bell Scott, and Barbara Smith (eds.), *All the Women Are White, All the Blacks are Men, But Some of Us Are Brave: Black Women's Studies* (The Feminist Press, 1982); Audre Lorde, 'The Master's Tools Will Never Dismantle The Master's House' in *Sister Outsider* (2019 [1984]), 103–106; Angela Davis, 'Racism, Birth Control and Reproductive Rights' in *Women, Race & Class* (Penguin Books, 2019 [1981]), 182–199. In Australia, for example: Aileen Moreton Robinson, *Talkin' Up to the White Women: Indigenous Women and Feminism* (University of Queensland Press, 2000), 107. The UK, for example: Valerie Amos and Pratibha Parmar, 'Challenging Imperial Feminism', *Feminist Review* no. 80 (2005 [1984]): 44–63.

7 Hemmings, *Considering Emma Goldman*, 5, 13, 80–124; Loretta J. Ross, *Calling In: How to Make Change with Those You'd Rather Cancel* (Simon & Schuster, 2025).

8 Christopher Castiglia, 'Critiquiness', *English Language Notes* 52, no. 2 (2013): 79.

NOTES TO CHAPTER 1

1 Kristin L. Hoganson, *The Heartland: An American History (*Penguin, 2019), xiv. On the African American experience in St. Joseph see, for example: 'In Their Own Words: An Oral History of African Americans in St. Joseph, MO', The Black Archives Museum, St. Joseph.

2 Beth Bailey, *Sex in the Heartland* (Harvard University Press, 1999), 25.

3 Rickie Solinger, *Wake Up Little Susie: Single Pregnancy and Race Before Roe* (Routledge, 1992); Ann Fessler, *The Girls Who Went Away: The Hidden History of Women Who Surrendered Children for Adoption in the Decades Before Roe v. Wade* (Penguin, 2006).

4 Leslie J. Reagan, *When Abortion Was a Crime: Women, Medicine, and Law in the United States 1867–1973* (University of California Press, 1997), 164.

5 Wini Breines, *Young, White and Miserable: Growing Up Female in the Fifties* (University of Chicago Press, 1992), 84–127.

6 'The Writing Life: A Talk Between Arthur M. Schlesinger Jr. and Jacques Barzun', in *Los Angeles Times Book Review*, May 21, 2000, 3–4.

7 Sophie Smith, 'Women and Intellectual History in the Twentieth Century, Part One: Rethinking the "Origins" of US Intellectual History,' *Journal of the History of Ideas* 85, no. 3 (2024): 425–454.

8 Michael Callahan, 'A Study of Female Sexuality', *Airmail News*, October 24, 2020.

9 I am indebted to Amia Srinivasan's careful treatment of porn in *The Right to Sex* (Bloomsbury, 2021).

10 For example, Andrea Dworkin, *Right Wing Women* (Penguin: 2025 [1983]), 212–216; Katherine McKinnon, 'Sexuality, Pornography

and Method: "Pleasure Under Patriarchy"', *Ethics* 99, no. 2 (1989): 314–346. See the work of the philosopher Rosa Vince on the limits of the focus on porn: 'After Objectification: Locating Harm', *Applied Philosophy* 41, no. 3 (2024): 442–462.

11 Carolyn Steedman, 'Enforced narratives: Stories of another self' in Tess Coslett, Celia Lury, and Penny Summerfield (eds.), *Feminism & Autobiography: Texts, Theories, Methods* (Routledge: 2002), 26–39.

12 On abortion: Maggie Doherty, 'The Abortion Stories We Tell', *Yale Review,* June 24, 2022; on trans health care see the cult zine *Mascara and Hope*, TransHealthUK, (2013); Shon Faye, *The Transgender Issue: An Argument for Justice* (Penguin, 2021).

NOTES TO CHAPTER 2

1 Anita Shreve, *Women Together, Women Alone: Seven Women Recall How the Women's Movement Changed Their Life and Their Time* (Ballantine Books, 1989), 5.

2 On women of colour and consciousness raising see, for example: Shirley Geok-lin Lim, 'Ain't I a Feminist: Reforming the Circle' in Blau DuPlessis and Snitow (eds.), *The Feminist Memoir Project,* 450–466; Brian Norman, 'The Consciousness-Raising Document, Feminist Anthologies, and Black Women in "Sisterhood Is Powerful"', *Frontiers: A Journal of Women Studies* 27, no. 3 (2006): 38–64.

3 Kathy Sarachild, 'A Programme for Feminist "Consciousness Raising",' in Shulamith Firestone and Anne Koedt (eds.), *Notes from the Second Year* 1970, 78–81. Duke University Digital Repository.

4 Marilyn Zwieg, '"Is Women's Liberation a Therapy Group"', in the Radical Therapist Collective (eds.), *The Radical Therapist* (Ballantine Books, 1971), 160–163.

5 Helen Garner quoted in Kath Kenny, *Staging a Revolution: When Betty Rocked the Pram* (Upswell, 2022), 20.

6 Katherine Turk, *The Women of NOW: How Feminists Built an Organization That Transformed America* (Farrar, Straus and Giroux, 2023).

7 Cynthia Eller, *The Myth of Matriarchal Prehistory: Why an Invented Past Will Not Give Women a Future* (Beacon Press, 2000).

8 Anne Koedt, 'Myth of the Vaginal Orgasm', *Notes from the First Year*, eds. New York Radical Women, June 1968, 11. Duke University Online Repository.

9 Muriel Fox, *The Women's Revolution: How We Changed Your Life* (Village Press, 2024), 260–261.

10 Smithsonian American Women's History Museum, *Sidedoor* podcast, season 11, episode 2.

11 Fox, *Women's Revolution*, 130–131; Debra Michals, 'The Buck Stops Where? 1970s Feminist Credit Unions, Women's Banks and the Gendering of Money', *Business and Economic History Online* 16 (2018): 1–13.

12 Jane Gerhard, 'Revisiting "The Myth of the Vaginal Orgasm": The Female Orgasm in American Sexual Thought and Second Wave Feminism', *Feminist Studies* 26, no. 2 (2000): 449–475.

13 Sigmund Freud, 'The Transformations of Puberty' in *Three Essays on Sexuality and Other Works* (Penguin, 1991 [1905, 1953 first English translation], 141–144.

14 Katherine Angel, 'The History of "Female Sexual Dysfunction" as a mental disorder in the 20th century', *Current Opinion in Psychiatry* 23, no. 6 (2010): 536–541; Jane F. Gerhard, *Desiring Revolution*.

15 Helen Deutsch, *The Psychology of Women* quoted in Gerhard, *Desiring Revolution*, 36–7.

16 Shulamith Firestone, *The Dialectic of Sex: The Case for Feminist Revo-*

lution (Verso, 2015 [1970]), 72; Betty Friedan, *The Feminine Mystique* (W. W. Norton, 2013[1963]), 103, 122–24, 182.

17 Sarah Chaney, *Am I Normal: The 200-Year Search for Normal People (and Why They Don't Exist)* (Profile, 2022), 272–73; Gerhard, *Desiring Revolution*, 53–64.

18 Kevan Wylie, 'Masters & Johnson—their Unique Contribution to Sexology', *BJPsych Advances* 28 (2022): 163–165; Gerhard, *Desiring Revolution*, 63–67.

19 William Masters and Virginia Johnson, *Human Sexual Response* (Little, Brown and Company, 1966), 6.

20 Adam Bernstein, 'William Masters, 85, dies: Pioneering Sex Researcher', *Washington Post*, February 19, 2001, B7.

21 Alex Comfort, *The Joy of Sex: A Gourmet Guide to Lovemaking* (Simon and Schuster, 1972), 199, 196, 13.

22 Jo Doezema, *Sex Slaves and Discourse Masters: The Construction of Trafficking* (Zed Books, 2010); Julia Laite, *The Disappearance of Lydia Harvey: A True Story of Sex, Crime and the Meaning of Justice* (Profile Books, 2021), 127–32; Ana Stevenson, 'The Gender-Apartheid Analogy in the Transnational Feminist Imaginary: *Ms. Magazine* and the Feminist Majority Foundation, 1972–2002,' *Safundi: The Journal of South African and American Studies* 19, no. 1 (2018): 93–116.

23 Ti-Grace Atkinson, *Amazon Odyssey* (Links Books, 1974), 5–7; On coerced performance and dance in North American slavery see Katrina Dyonne Thompson, *Ring Shout, Wheel About: The Racial Politics of Music and Dance in North American Slavery* (University of Illinois Press, 2016), 69-98.

24 Echols, *Daring to be Bad,* 10.

25 Angela Davis, *Women, Race and Class* (Penguin, 2019 [1981]), 155–182.

26 Srinivasan, *The Right to Sex,* 14–15; Michele Wallace, *Black Macho*

and the Myth of the Superwoman (Verso, 1990).

27 Lola Olufemi, *Feminism, Interrupted: Disrupting Power* (Pluto Press, 2020), 96–99; Katherine Angel, *Tomorrow Sex Will Be Good Again: Women and Desire in the Age of Consent* (Verso, 2021), 1–40.

28 Adrienne Rich, 'Compulsory Heterosexuality and Lesbian Existence', *Signs: Journal of Women in Culture and Society* 5, no. 4 (1980): 631–660.

29 Ruth Rosen, *The World Split Open*, 83.

30 Radicalesbians, 'The Woman Identified Woman', 1970, Digital Scholars at Rochester University.

NOTES TO CHAPTER 3

1 John Berger, *Ways of Seeing* (London: Penguin, 1972), 46.

2 Peter Crye and Elizabeth Stephens, *Normality: A Critical Genealogy* (University of Chicago Press, 2017); also: Chaney, *Am I Normal.*

3 Eric Kaufman, *Whiteshift: Populism, Immigration and the Future of White Majorities* (Abrams Press, 2019), 371.

4 Lord Ashcroft, '"This is what happens when you get normal people like us and no-one listens to them": My latest focus groups', *Lord Ashcroft Polls,* August 19, 2025.

5 Michael Warner, *Fear of a Queer Planet* (University of Minnesota Press, 1993), xxvii; Laura Doan, *Disturbing Practices: History, Sexuality, and Women's Experience of Modern War* (University of Chicago Press, 2013), 169; Crye and Stephens, *Normality*, 6–8.

6 For example: bell hooks, *Ain't I a Woman: Black Women and Feminism* (Routledge, 2014 [1981]); Hazel Carby, 'White Woman listen! Black feminism and the boundaries of sisterhood' in the Centre for

Contemporary Cultural Studies (eds.), *The Empire Strikes Back: Race and Racism in 70s Britain* (Routledge, 1982), 212–35.

7 Roberta Perkins quoted in Rebecca Sheehan, 'Settler Colonialism in Black and White: Roberta Sykes, Germaine Greer, and the Different Embodied Experiences of Womanhood, Rape, and Sovereignty', *Signs: A Journal of Women in Culture and Society,* 49:4 (2024), 731–754, 736.

8 Frances M. Beal, 'Double Jeopardy: To Be Black and Female' in Robin Morgan, *Sisterhood is Powerful: An Anthology of Writings from the Women's Liberation Movement* (Vintage Books, 1970), 340-353.; Linda La Rue, 'The Black Movement and Women's Liberation', *The Black Scholar* 1, No.7 (1970), 36-42.

9 Srinivasan, *The Right to Sex,* 103–104.

10 Robin Zheng, 'Why Yellow Fever Isn't Flattering: A Case Against Racial Fetishes', *Journal of the American Philosophical Association* 2, no. 3 (2016): 400–419.

11 Alice Walker, '"Women of Color" Have Rarely Had the Opportunity to Write About Their Love Affairs', in Hannah Dawson, *The Penguin Book of Feminist Writing* (Penguin, 2021), 279–282

12 Martha C. Nussbaum, 'Objectification', *Philosophy & Public Affairs* 24, no. 4 (1995): 249–91, 257.

13 Martha Shelley, 'Subversion in the Womans Movement', *Gay Liberation Forum* 1, no. 7 (1970).

NOTES TO CHAPTER 4

1 A. G. Hopkins, *American Empire: A Global History* (Princeton University Press, 2018), 720.

2 Victoria De Grazia, *Irresistible Empire: America's Advance Through 20th Century Europe* (Harvard University Press, 2005), 3.

3 On imperialist feminism see, for example: Vron Ware, *Beyond the Pale: White Women, Racism and History* (Verso, 1992); Chandra Mohanty, 'Under Western Eyes: Feminist Scholarship and Colonial Discourses', *boundary 2* 12, no. 3 (1984): 333–358; Valerie Amos and Pratibha Parmar, Challenging Imperial Feminism', *Feminist Review* 17 no. 1 (1984): 3–19; Antoinette Burton, *Burdens of History: British Feminism, Indian Women and Imperial Culture, 1865–1915* (University of North Carolina Press, 1994); Rafia Zakaria, *Against White Feminism* (Penguin, 2021).

4 Kathy Davis, *The Making of Our Bodies, Ourselves* (Duke University Press, 2007), 150.

5 George Orwell, *1984,* (Oxford University Press, 2021 [1949]), 238.

6 Kristen R. Ghodsee, *Why Women have Better Sex Under Socialism: And Other Arguments for Economic Independence, (Bold Type Books, 2018),* 137.

7 Josie McLellan, *Love in the Time of Communism: Intimacy and Sexuality in the GDR* (Cambridge University Press, 2011).

8 John Dower quoted in Mire Koikari, 'Exporting Democracy? American Women, "Feminist Reforms", and the Politics of Imperialism in the U.S. Occupation of Japan, 1945–1952', *Frontiers: A Journal of Women Studies* 23, no. 1 (2002): 23–45, 26.

9 Lindesay Parrott, 'Out of Feudalism: Japan's Women', *New York Times*, October 28, 1945, 10.

10 Meghan Warner Mettler, 'Modern Butterfly: American Percep-

tions of Japanese Women and their Role in International Relations, 1945–1960', *Journal of Women's History* 26, no. 4 (2014): 60–82, 61.

11 Setsu Shigematsu, *Scream from the Shadows: The Women's Liberation Movement in Japan* (University of Minnesota Press, 2012), xxxii, 151.

12 Tanaka Mitsu, trans. Setsu Shigematsu, 'Liberation from the Toilet–1970', Salar Mohandesi, Bjarke Skærlund Risanger, and Laurence Cox (eds.), *Voices of 1968: Documents from the Global North* (Pluto, 2019), 136.

13 Simone de Beauvoir, trans. Constance Borde and Sheila Malovany-Chevallier, *The Second Sex* (Vintage, 2011 [1949]), 373.

14 Herbert S. Klein and Francisco Vidal Luna, *Brazil , 1964–1985: Military Regimes of Latin America and the Cold War* (Yale University Press, 2017), 51.

15 Sonia E. Alvarez, *Engendering Democracy in Brazil: Women's Movements and Transition Politics* (Princeton University Press,1990), 5.

16 Tracey Panek, 'Celebrating 50 Years of LS&Co. in Brazil' July 11, 2022, *Levi Strauss & Co.*

17 Biju Belinky, 'How Cake Became a Form of Resistance Under Brazil's Military Dictatorship', *Vice*, January 17, 2019. Sandra Reimao, (translated by Juliet Attwater) 'Repression and Resistance Under the Military Dictatorship', PhD thesis, University of Sao Paulo, 2011, 5

18 Paolo Marconi quoted in Reimao, 'Repression and Resistance', 34.

19 Aline Rubin, Belinda Mandelbaum, and Stephen Frosh, 'No memory, no desire': Psychoanalysis in Brazil during repressive times', *Psychoanalysis and History* 18, no. 1 (2016): 93–118.

20 Lila Abu-Lughod, *Do Muslim Women Need Saving* (Harvard University Press, 2013), 115, 127.

21 Fran Hosken, *The Hosken Report: The Sexual and Genital Mutilation of*

Females (Women's International Network News, 1979), 7-8.

22 Awa Thiam, *Speak Out, Black Sisters: Feminism and Oppression in Black Africa* (Pluto, 1986), 15.

23 Adi Gevins, 'Tackling Tradition: African Women Speak Out Against Female Circumcision', Miranda Davies (ed.), *Third World, Second Sex* vol. 2 (Zed, 1983), 244-249, 244.

24 AAWORD, 'A Statement on Genital Mutilation', Miranda Davies (ed.), *Third World, Second Sex* vol. 1 (Zed, 1983), 217-220, 219.

25 Alex Gilandas, *Sex and the Single Filipina: The Omega Woman* (Philippine Education Co., 1982).

26 Adrienne Rich, *Blood, Bread and Poetry: Selected Prose 1979–1985*, (W.W.Norton, 1986), 156.

27 Rafia Zakaria, 'White Feminists Wanted to Invade', *The Nation*, August 17, 2021.

28 http://www.rawa.org/us-strikes.htm

NOTES TO CHAPTER 5

1 R.W. Connell, *Masculinities* (Polity, 1995), 226

2 Michael A. Messner, 'The limits of the "Male Sex Role": An analysis of Men's Liberation and Men's Right Movements' Discourse', *Gender & Society* 12, no. 3 (June 1998): 255–276, 256.

3 Susan Brownmiller, *In Our Time: Memoir of a Revolution* (Delta, 1999), 17–18.

4 Alice Echols, *Daring to Be Bad,* 49.

5 Brother, 'Stop Playboying' in Jon Snodgrass (ed.), *For Men Against Sexism: A Book of Readings* (Times Change Press, 1977), 114–116, 116.

6 On men's liberation see: Lucy Delap, 'Feminism, Masculinities and Emotional Politics in Late Twentieth Century Britain', *Cultural and Social History* 14, no. 5 (2018): 571–593; Louise Bachaud, 'US Men's

Liberation in the 1970s: Autopsy of a Movement' *The Journal of Men's Studies,* 2025.

7 Marc Feigen Fasteau, *The Male Machine* (Delta, 1975), 1–2.

8 Warren Farrell, *The Liberated Man* (Bantam, 1975), xxix, 5.

9 de Beauvoir, *The Second Sex,* 709.

10 On celibacy see, for example the journal by Boston-based feminist group Cell 16, *No More Fun and Games,* Duke University Repository. On lesbian separatism see, for example: Jill Johnson, *Lesbian Nation: The Feminist Solution* (Simon and Schuster, 1973); Rich, 'Compulsory Heterosexuality and Lesbian Existence', 631-660.

11 Linda J. Waite, *US Women at Work* (The Rand Corporation: 1981), iv.

12 'Women of the Year: Great Changes, New Chances, Tough Choices', *Time*, January 1976, 6.

13 Robert W Bednarzik and Stephen M. St. Marie, 'Employment and unemployment in 1976', *Monthly Labor Review February*, 1977, 3–1, 11.

14 bell hooks, *The Will to Change: Men, Masculinity and Love* (Washington Square Press, 2004), 39.

15 Ruby Hamad, *White Tears, Brown Scars* (Melbourne University Press, 2019); Terese Jonsson, *Innocent Subjects: Feminism and Whiteness* (Pluto Press, 2020).

16 Nova Reid, 'No More White Saviours, Thanks: How to be a true anti-racist ally', *The Guardian*, 2021, https://www.theguardian.com/world/2021/sep/19no-more-white-saviours-thanks-how-to-be-a-true-anti-racist-ally.

17 Faludi, *Backlash*, 89.

18 Patrice Taddonio, '"All About the Fight": How Donald Trump Developed His Political Playbook', September 24, 2024, PBS.

19 Kristen Kobes Du Mez, *Jesus and John Wayne: How White Evangelicals Corrupted a Faith and Fractured a Nation* (Liveright, 2020), 20.

20 Jerry Falwell, *Listen America!* (Bantam, 1981), 130.

21 Marjorie J. Spruill, *Divided We Stand: The Battle Over Women's Rights and Family Values that Polarized American Politics* (Bloomsbury, 2017); Emily Suzanne Johnson, *This is Our Message: Women's Leadership in the Christian Right* (Cambridge University Press, 2019).

22 Phyllis Schlafly, *The Power of the Positive Woman* (Arlington House, 1977), 16.

23 Beverley and Tim LaHaye, *The Act of Marriage: The Beauty of Sexual Love* (Zondervan Publishing House, 1976), 73; Kobes Du Mez, *Jesus and John Wayne*, 60–73; 89–93.

24 Warren Farrell quoted in Faludi, *Backlash*, 334.

25 Warren Farrell, *Why Men Are the Way They Are* (Berkley Books, 1986), 24, 203; Warren Farrell, *The Myth of Male Power: Why Men Are the Disposable Sex* (Simon & Schuster, 1993), 16,21.

26 Laura Bates, *Men Who Hate Women: The Extremism Nobody Is Talking About* (Simon & Schuster, 2020), 119.

27 Jamie Tahsin and Matt Shea, *Clown World: Four Years Inside Andrew Tate's Manosphere* (Quercus, 2024), 9.

28 Michael Kimmel quoted in Mariah Blake, 'Mad Men: Inside the Men's Rights Movement—and the Army of Misogynists and Trolls It Spawned', *Mother Jones*, January/February 2015.

29 Andrew Tate quoted in Tahsin and Shea, *Clown World*, 12.

30 Warren Farrell quoted in Blake, 'Mad Men: Inside the Men's Rights Movement'.

NOTES TO CHAPTER 6

1 'The Feminists: A Political Organization to Annihilate Sex Roles', in *Notes from the Second Year*, 114–118.

2 David Spiegelhalter, *Sex by Numbers: What Statistics Can Tell Us About Sexual Behaviour* (Profile, 2015), 40.
3 Tiffany Watt Smith, *Bad Friend: A Century of Revolutionary Friendships* (Faber, 2025), 245.
4 Sara B. Raley, Marybeth J. Mattingly, and Suzanne M. Bianchi, 'How Dual are Dual-Income Couples? Documenting Change from 1970 to 2001', *Journal of Marriage and Family* 68, No. 1, 11–28.
5 As it is in other feminist work that thinks through violence, see: Zora Simic, 'Seeing the Signs: Thinking historically about coercive control', *Women's History Review*, 2025): 1–24.
6 See, for example: Alice Echols, 'Cultural Feminism: Feminist Capitalism and the Anti-Pornography Movement', *Social Text*, no. 7 (Spring–Summer 1983): 34–50; Johanna Brenner, 'Beyond Essentialism: Feminist Theory and Strategy in the Peace Movement', *Verso Blog*, December 8, 2016.
7 Kimberlé Crenshaw, 'Demarginalizing the Intersection of Race and Sex: A Black Feminist Critique of Antidiscrimination Doctrine, Feminist Theory and Antiracist Politics', *University of Chicago Legal Forum* 1, no. 8 (1989): 139–167; Important prehistories to intersectionality can be found in the work of Claudia Jones, Angela Davis, The Combahee River Collective, The Third World Women's Alliance, and Patricia Hill Collins.
8 Brent D. Ryan and Daniel Campo, 'Autopia's End: The Decline and Fall of Detroit's automotive manufacturing industry', *Journal of Planning History* 12, no. 2 (May 1, 2013): 95–132.
9 Faludi, *Backlash,* 27–32.
10 Kobes Du Mez, *Jesus and John Wayne*, 88.
11 Lynn Hecht Schafran, 'Reagan Vs. Women', *New York Times*, October 13, 1981.

12 Quinn Slobodian, *Hayek's Bastards: Race, Gold, IQ, and the Capitalism of the Far Right* (Zone Books, 2025), 10.

13 Emily Johnson, *This Is Our Message: Women's Leadership in the Christian Right* (Oxford University Press, 2019), 1.

14 Rosemary Thomson quoted in Spruill, *Divided We Stand*, 93.

15 Spruill, *Divided We Stand*, 187.

16 Brenda Feigen, *Not One of the Boys: Living Life as a Feminist* (Penguin, 2000), 123.

17 Andrea Dworkin, *Right Wing Women* (Penguin, 2024 [1983]), 24.

18 Phyllis Schlafly, 'What's Wrong with "Equal Rights" for Women? – 1972', Archives of Women's Political Communication, Iowa State University.

19 Fox executive and Michael Douglas quoted in Faludi, *Backlash,* 141, 150.

20 Faludi, *Backlash,* 380.

21 Monika Lewinsky, 'The Price of Shame', Archives of Women's Political Communication, Iowa State University.

22 Anita Miller (ed.), *The Complete Transcripts of the Clarence Thomas - Anita Hill Hearings: October 11, 12, 13, 1991* (Academy Chicago Publishers, 1994), 68–69, 117; Ming-Qi Chu, 'Why We Need Anita Hill', *LA Review of Books,* September 20, 2014.

23 Joanna Bourke, *Rape: A History from 1860 to the Present Day* (Virago, 2007), 29.

NOTES TO EPILOGUE

1 Louis Bachaud and Sarah E. Jones, 'The Use and Misuse of Evolutionary Psychology in Online Manosphere Communities: The Case of Female Mating Strategies', *Evolutionary Human Sciences*, 5,

e28 (2023, 1-15; Rebecca L. Stotzer and Ashley Nelson, 'The (Anti) Feminism of Trad Wives', *Terrorism and Political Violence*, 2025, 1–14.

2 Jessica Winter, 'J.D. Vance's Sad, Strange Politics of the Family', *New Yorker*, July 25, 2024.

3 Nic Murray and Rajeev Syal, 'Two in Five Arrested for Last Summers Riots had been Reported for Domestic Abuse', *The Guardian,* 26 July, 2025; ABC News, 'Trump Says He'll Protect Women "Whether the women like it or not"', October 31, 2024.

4 Faye, *The Transgender Issue.*

5 Dworkin, *Right Wing Women*, 22.

6 Jody R. Herman and Andrew R. Flores, 'Safety and Privacy in Public Restrooms and Other Gendered Facilities', February 2025, UCLA Williams Institute; Stop the ERA pamphlet, Florida Memory: State Library and Archives of Florida; Neil J. Young, 'The Decades-Old Roots of Houston's Bathroom Panic', *Slate,* November 4, 2015.

7 Tradwife quoted in Stotzer and Nelson, 'The (Anti)Feminism of Trad Wives', 7.

8 Kristen Ghodsee, 'Tradwives Are the Harbingers of Systemic Breakdown', *Jacobin*, April 27, 2025.

9 Gil Troy, *Morning in America: How Ronald Reagan Invented the '80s* (Princeton University Press, 2013), 8.